PRAISE FOR *GRANT WRITING*

"The authors provide a much-needed, tailored approach for faculty, scholars, researchers, and other professionals to understanding grant writing. This book will provide a positive contribution to the field."—David H. Lindeman, CFRE, GPC, Co-Editor, *Journal of the Grant Professionals Association*, President, Global Grant Solutions, LLC Washington, DC

"A treasure trove of information for anyone interested in pursuing grants."—Charles J. Russo, EdD, JD, Panzer Chair in Education, University of Dayton

"Grant writing is both a science and an art. Rajan and Tomal have not only written a valuable and engaging resource for grant writers who want to learn how to write grants, but have given us a resource for institutional leaders who want to help their faculty generate grants."—Robert K. Wilhite, EdD, Professor and Chair, Department of Leadership, Concordia University Chicago

"What Jean Francois Champollion was to deciphering Egyptian hieroglyphs Rajan and Tomal are to grant writing. They know the process inside and out. They explain it in a way to remove the fear and mystery. This book is a great read for anyone who wants to understand what can be an arcane and secretive process."—Fenwick W. English, R. Wendell Eaves Sr. Distinguished Professor of Educational Leadership, University of North Carolina at Chapel Hill

"Individuals who have the ability to write successful grant proposals are well-respected and valued in organizations today. This comprehensive, timely, and well-written book should be a mainstay to all who seek to be effective grant writers."—Carol J. Reiseck, EdD, Assistant Dean, Learning Technology and Innovation, Concordia University Chicago

"The authors provide a comprehensive, clear, and cohesive step-by-step process for understanding grant writing from start to finish. This is an excellent guide for scholars and practitioners, as well as a helpful text for students in a variety of fields. I know there will always be a space on my desk for this important work."—Azadeh F. Osanloo MPA, PhD, Stan Fulton Endowed Chair in Education, New Mexico State University

"A great resource! This book provides clear and creative approaches to improve your grant writing. It is an interesting and useful read and great for scholars looking to improve their grant writing."—Christopher S. Reigstad, PhD, Associate Professor of Biology, Concordia University Chicago

"In a time of decreasing revenues, Rajan and Tomal provide a practical guide to finding grant opportunities and applying for them."—Craig A. Schilling, EdD, Advisor, Digital Schools LLC, Salinas, California

"This comprehensive book is not only a valuable resource for grant writers who want to learn how to write grants, faculty who want to secure grants, but it can also be a resource for institutional leaders who want to help their faculty get grants. The accessible, yet scholarly, information reflects the authors' vast experience—well done!"—Beth Venzke, Professor of Psychology, Concordia University Chicago

"Authors Rekha Rajan and Dan Tomal are scholars and experienced grant writers who provide a unique perspective on the field. This book is an essential, effective, and accessible read for anyone who wants to secure a grant. I wish such a book had been available when I wrote my first grant years ago."—Carol R. Melnick, PhD, Professor Emerita, National-Louis University, Illinois

"Schools everywhere are struggling for increasing limited resources. The authors provide valuable information to those tasked with finding and securing the grants they need to improve their schools. This is an excellent resource for current and aspiring school leaders who want to gain a comprehensive understanding of the grant writing process."—Jeffrey T. Brierton, PhD, Associate Professor of Educational Leadership, Concordia University Chicago

"This book is not only a valuable resource for grant writers who want to learn how to write grants, but it can also be a resource for institutional leaders who want to help their faculty get grants and for seasoned grant writers who may need a refresher in certain knowledge areas."—Susan Brittain, MAE, Member of Grants Professional Association

"This book is not only a valuable resource for grant writers who want to learn how to write grants, but also as a resource for institutional leaders who want to help their faculty get grants."—Brenda F. Graham, Professor, Department of Leadership, Concordia University Chicago

"Practical book written to improve the grant writing skills of people. I highly recommend this book."—Dr. Christopher G. Pritchett, Associate Professor, Instructional Leadership and Administration, Troy University, Alabama

"Without minimizing the complexity of the grant writing process, Rajan and Tomal have achieved the perfect balance by providing the novice with a solid foundation in the basic essential tools of grant writing while also providing the experienced grant writer with an abundance of advanced techniques. This extremely practical guide is perfect for anyone needing or wanting more money in their professional budget. This book is sure to become your most used grant writing reference."—Heather Anne Harder, PhD, Associate Professor of Graduate and Innovative Programs, Concordia University Chicago

OTHER BOOKS IN THE SERIES

Action Research for Educators
Action Research for Educators, Second Edition
Challenging Students to Learn: How to Use Effective Leadership and Motivation Tactics
Discipline by Negotiation: Methods for Managing Student Behavior
How to Finish and Defend Your Dissertation: Strategies to Complete the Professional Practice Doctorate
Leading School Change: Maximizing Resources for School Improvement
Managing Human Resources and Collective Bargaining
Resource Management for School Administrators: Optimizing Fiscal, Facility, and Human Resources
The Teacher Leader: Core Competencies and Strategies for Effective Leadership
Technology and Online Learning for Educators
Ethics and Politics in School Leadership
Supervision and Evaluation for Learning and Growth

Grant Writing

Practical Strategies for Scholars and Professionals

Rekha S. Rajan and Daniel Tomal

ROWMAN & LITTLEFIELD
Lanham • Boulder • New York • London

Published by Rowman & Littlefield
A wholly owned subsidiary of The Rowman & Littlefield Publishing Group, Inc.
4501 Forbes Boulevard, Suite 200, Lanham, Maryland 20706
www.rowman.com

Unit A, Whitacre Mews, 26-34 Stanuary Street, London SE11 4AB

British Library Cataloguing in Publication Information Available

Library of Congress Cataloging-in-Publication Data Available

ISBN 978-1-4758-1440-8 (hardcover)
ISBN 978-1-4758-1441-5 (paperback)
ISBN 978-1-4758-1442-2 (e-book)

∞™ The paper used in this publication meets the minimum requirements of American National Standard for Information Sciences—Permanence of Paper for Printed Library Materials, ANSI/NISO Z39.48-1992.

"Money speaks sense in a language all nations understand."

—Aphra Behn

Contents

Foreword

The book by Rekha Rajan, EdD, and Daniel Tomal, PhD, is the first of its kind. The authors have taken a subject that is frequently avoided and addressed it in a nonthreatening and expert way. They unabashedly acknowledge that notwithstanding advanced degrees in the arts, humanities, science, or education, many professionals lack the skills necessary to write a successful grant application. It is not uncommon for most professionals to lack basic knowledge of grant writing—or at least how to translate the skills of their discipline into being a successful grant writer.

It's OK that not everyone knows how to write a grant. It would be great if there was a grant writer on your staff who handled the grant process so you could focus on the research project or whatever purpose the grant was intended to fund. However, we all know this is not the reality most of the time.

The authors come from a position of authority in this regard; that is, they both have advanced degrees and through their experiences discovered they were at a sizable disadvantage because the skills perfected in their particular disciplines did not automatically help them to write a successful grant proposal. With that in mind, they put this book together to outline what they learned and to help others who are confronted with the same challenge to overcome the obstacles that professionals face when asked (or required) to handle the grant funding in addition to the project.

The book is easy to read from beginning to end. Or you can jump around to subjects as you need them. The authors have arranged the book in chapters, each of which focuses on a different aspect of the grant writing process, from grant research to grant management. Rekha and

Dan are also both musicians. They have taken their musical proclivity and cleverly analogized grant writing to an orchestral performance, from the Overture (Introduction to Grants); Exposition (Finding the Grants); Theme and Variations (Developing the Proposal); Recapitulation (Completing the Proposal); Finale (Revising and Editing the Proposal); and the Encore (Beyond the Proposal).

The resulting flow and informality make the book a pleasure to read. It presents grant writing in clear and concise language without being condescending. Grant writing terms are defined. Real life experiences are related. Each chapter ends with a "Notation" section and a "Reflections" section, giving the reader quick reference to the contents of the chapter.

The authors take the position that it is worth the effort to put the time into learning subtle grant writing techniques as distinguished from a professional's usual scholarly work product. This is more than a "How-To" book. It is written to an audience in whom certain skills are presumed, but who may lack the knowledge to make writing a successful grant more than following some "magic formula."

Connecting the musical analogy presented by the authors to the grant writing that I personally conduct (pun?), I am prompted to recollect my own musical background as a pianist. I am a fan of Johann Sebastian Bach's compositions written as exercises and instruction for his son. We know these as "Two-Part Inventions." They're difficult to play because one hand is going one way and the other hand is going another way, but they both seem to be playing sort of the same thing and eventually end up in the same place. It sounds as if the notes come and go in different directions, but always seem to coalesce in a balanced way.

This musical counterpoint (contrapuntal) mode is easily juxtaposed with grant writing. The ebb and flow of the process—from grant research to award management—sometimes feels like it goes off in different directions yet always has the same end point. Advance planning and focused effort are the infrastructure of the successful grant.

Rekha Rajan and Dan Tomal are both scholars and published authors with a wealth of knowledge and experience, which they have presented in this book. Their work is recognized nationally, and they have broken new ground with this book. There are differences that all professionals must know before they can write a successful grant proposal.

This book will explain the differences.

Andrew S. Rawdon, JD
Co-Editor—*Journal of the Grant Professionals Association*
Director of Development—Compeer Rochester, Inc.
Fairport, NY
January 18, 2015

Authors' Note

There are many languages spoken in our diverse world. However, regardless of culture, background, or country, there are two universal languages: *music* and *money*.

Music is often considered a universal language in that you do not need to have studied music or trained for years as a professional in order to appreciate, value, or understand what music tries to communicate. While we both value music, we have different musical backgrounds. I spent nearly a decade training as a classical vocalist and performing in musical theater, while Dan, with only limited professional musical training, can play a ripping homage to the Beatles on his electric guitar.

Our appreciation of music inspired us to create a thread throughout this book, to envision how composing a symphony—the grandest of all classical musical compositions—is equivalent in many ways to writing a grant proposal. It symbolizes the greatest achievement, for an artist *and* scholar.

When you set out to compose a symphony, you may begin with one melodic line that builds into the overture—the theme, the tone of the musical piece. These ideas are referenced throughout your work, recalled and anticipated at cadences and codas, manipulated in themes and variations, and referenced in a recapitulation. For some musicians, symphonies can take years to compose, while others can write their musical ideas in months.

Grant writing is an important, evolving field. It requires tireless revision and editing, collaboration, and compromise to achieve the goal—*get the money*. In many ways, writing a grant is for a scholar or professional, as composing a symphony is for a musician. Grant writing requires the same expansion of a single idea—building a reciprocal relationship with peers, finding harmony with funders.

—RSR

Acknowledgments

There are many people who helped shape our ideas—both musically and academically—and we are grateful for this support, expertise, and inspiration. This book is dedicated to our colleagues at Concordia University Chicago who have provided feedback, comments, and encouragement. And, to the students enrolled in the masters in grant writing, management, and evaluation program, whose innovative ideas will compose the future of grant writing and program evaluation.

We would like to thank the important people in our lives: Rekha's husband, Kumar Bharat Rajan, PhD, and their three young children, Jagan Rajan, Madhavi Rajan, and Arjun Rajan; and Dan's wife and children, Annette Tomal, PhD, Jonathan (and Sarah) Tomal, BA, Stephanie Tomal, JD, and Justin Tomal, MD.

It's not over until the fat lady sings…

1

Overture

An Introduction to Grants

Imagine a room full of professionals from a variety of fields: arts educators, educational leadership, health care managers, university faculty members, directors of not-for-profits, educational outreach program managers, scientists, math teachers, and students. Imagine yourself in that room.

Then one person enters who is a grant writing specialist. Naturally, everyone in the room, including you, will have a question for the grant writer. You may be drawn to find out what information the grant writer has, how that information can help to get grants, and with what contacts or organizations has the grant writer already built connections. What questions would you ask?

Grant writing is an important, ever-changing field. Since the evolution of small businesses, the developments of universities, and the support of scholarly research, partnerships, and programs, we have needed grants. Why? Simply, because securing a grant shows that what you are doing is important, innovative, exciting, and valued. For a small organization, securing a grant can make the difference in being able to provide valuable programming to the community. Likewise, a larger university might seek out private donors or endowments to be able to give scholarships to students in need.

For scholars, industry professionals, university faculty, consultants, and independent researchers, having a grant can mean a promotion, job security, or just the validation that the research you are doing is meaningful. In fact, securing grants and supporting individual research with external funding is often an expectation of holding a faculty position.

Reflect on your own work, perhaps even within your graduate education—regardless of your field of study; did you take any coursework specific to grant writing, budgeting, or grant management?

Scholars in a variety of disciplines have pursued excellence in education in various fields of study, dedicating countless hours of research, mentoring, collaboration, and teaching within a concentrated area of study. While the focus of the dissertations, research projects, or independent studies may vary, upon securing a faculty position, the unrealistic expectation is the same—individuals are often expected to know how to get grants without having any prior experience.

Grant writing as a separate and distinct profession is a relatively new field. While grant writing itself is not new, it is only for the past two decades that the grant profession has been recognized as a separate discipline (Blitch, 2012). The development of grant writing as a unique field is often recognized as an extension of fundraising efforts that eventually led to the need for grant writers and specialists. Along with this expansion came professional organizations, networking opportunities, and individuals who sought to identify themselves as grant writers with a code of ethics and professional membership (Janssen and Pearl, 2009).

Grant writers then began finding employment as consultants for not-for-profits, corporations, and universities. With this growth came a resurgence of interest in grant writing in supporting faculty positions and faculty research. Furthermore, as the number of tenure-track positions has begun to decline in higher education, there is a greater need for grant writing to become a part of the academic culture (Sridhar, 2009).

Many universities now have grants specialists who collaborate with faculty, assisting with managing the budget or building partnerships while the faculty principal investigator on the grant may be persuading colleagues, department chairs, and deans on the efficacy or necessity of their project (Einhorn, 2013). Even with the establishment of a grants center or office of faculty development, the pursuit of a grant is primarily the responsibility of the faculty member.

Let us revisit the opening vignette. What questions came to mind when presented with the opportunity to talk to a grants specialist? Most likely some of your questions included getting help with a project statement, narrowing or understanding a budget, finding some agencies to fund your next research project, or simply getting help with putting together a proposal.

While it is exciting and motivating to envision having research funded from an external source, grant writing can be a laborious, tiresome process, often filled with rejections far before finding out that you have been rewarded (and awarded!) for your hard work.

As a colleague once asked us, *what's the point in spending hours and hours writing a grant proposal, when I don't know if I'm going to be funded, and I could have published two papers instead!* The reality is that grant writing is not an exact field—you can never know when you will get a grant, or when the application you submit will be the one that will click.

WHO NEEDS THE MONEY?

So, is it really worth the effort? That is ultimately a question you have to ask yourself, for your own situation and context. A goal of many faculty members, researchers, and educators is to secure that one, first grant, regardless of the exact dollar amount. While some people pursue grants for support for individual research projects or innovative ideas, many faculty members are expected to *have* grants to support their position.

This book is written as a response to the large number of grant writing books that focus only on assisting not-for-profits, fundraising efforts, or presenting a "formula" for grant writing that in all reality does not exist. Grant writing is both a science and an art—it the process of knowing *what* to apply for and *how* to ask, building relationships, showing persistence, and being willing to revise, rewrite, and resubmit.

In that sense, grant writing shares many traits and qualities equated with being a good scholar. The proposal and project statement are similar to writing a research paper or project, a master's thesis, or dissertation. The idea is the same: finding an important issue or problem; stating the need for making it better; describing the process for how to examine, explore, investigate, or change that problem; and identifying the various individuals who will collaborate or participate to make that change.

Similarly, the grant writing process includes three basic dimensions: the grantee's needs, the funder's needs, and the organizational needs. The grantee's needs typically involve your personal time and vested interest in pursuing and receiving grants. This is also influenced by the amount of additional resources you have available within your setting and your collaborators.

The funder's needs often dictate what it is you will be applying for and how you will be applying for the grant. Is it a large funder or smaller, private foundation? What are the funder's goals, missions, and vision for their own agency? Funder's have their own specific needs that they want to meet every time they fund a project. Ensuring alignment between your own needs and those of the funder will strengthen your application.

The organizational needs are described within your university, institution, or organization's setting. Are you a faculty in a university or a professional managing a new, start-up not-for-profit? Are you a student

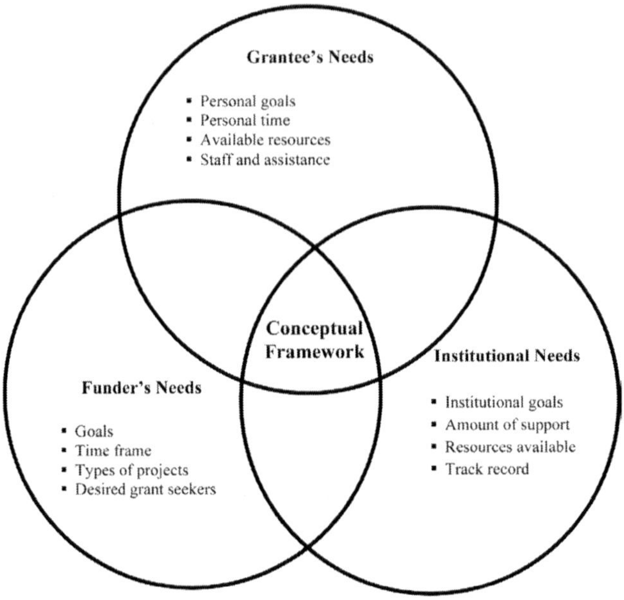

Figure 1.1. Grant Writing Conceptual Framework

trying to understand the world of grant writing, or an assistant director working on finding, writing, and submitting proposals? The needs of your organization will determine how much support you will receive, the resources that may be available to you during and after receiving an award, and any history of being awarded similar grants. We outline these dimensions and their overlapping fields in Figure 1.1, our Grant Writing Conceptual Framework.

Although there are many options for individuals trying to build their grant writing expertise, the reality is that many people are ultimately "left to their own devices when seeking the best path to a successful career" as a grant writer (Dillehay and Skinner, 2012, p. 73). There are many individuals who pursue additional coursework, certificate programs, or attend workshops and seminars that claim to "make you a grant writer" or teach you all the secrets to grant writing in a day. However, much more research is needed to determine if these popular venues and quick fixes in grant writing are truly effective.

Since grant writing was traditionally a discipline that grew from practical experience in the field, the large growth trajectories in the past decade and need for grant writers has demonstrated a growing interest in developing degree programs for the grants profession. There are many institutions that are moving away from the fast-track certificates and offering graduate degrees in grant writing and management.

These changes continue to support the development of grant writing as a separate profession, but they also provide opportunities for scholars to further their own understanding of grant writing. In fact, we know many individuals who after attaining their graduate degrees returned to school for further training and understanding of writing and managing grants.

Faculty have also developed individual courses (Sisk, 2011), as well as implemented different workshops or certificates to address a growing need for grant writers (O'Neal, 2008; Reynolds et al., 1998). These professional development opportunities continue to support the grants profession, providing background and educational experience to complement the vast amount of professional grant writing being conducted.

There is an ongoing debate in higher education on whether we can actually teach people to become scholarly writers. *Can you teach someone how to write a scholarly paper?* Or, is successful writing a result of practice coupled with a person's own innate writing abilities? Similarly, the question often remains on whether you can actually teach someone to be a good grant writer.

While most faculty members, researchers, and scholars are considered to be experts in one or more related fields, independent grant writers and professionals often have the task of being able to write grants across disciplines. This creates an advantage for scholars seeking grants as a majority of grants are subjected to a rigorous peer-review process by specialists in each field (Smith and Tremore, 2008).

We can all be better grant writers—and perhaps, even better *writers*—as this is what lies at the very foundation of grant writing. We constantly read, revise, and shape our own thoughts and ideas in our scholarly works, and grant writing is the same. It requires the ability to convey ideas concisely and clearly, to be succinct, and to emphasize the importance of a project. The key here is recognizing that grant writing is a skill—as with any field of study—and with practice, any individual can master the language of grant writing.

Some people, in fact, equate grant writing to "speaking" another language. If you have never written a grant before, trying to decipher what the RFP and LOI ask for (or even what they mean) is harder than deciding who the PI and Co-PI will be on the grant. So, before delving into where to look for grants, how to write the proposal, and working on assessment, let us uncover the language of grant writing. Table 1.1 presents some basic (and important) definitions of the various components of the grant writing process listed below:

Principal Investigator (PI). The *principal investigator* (PI) is the lead researcher on a grant proposal. This individual is primarily responsible for overseeing the goals and objectives of the grant, managing the budget, and ensuring that the purpose matches the outcomes. The PI typically has

Table 1.1. Grant Writing Terminology, Abbreviations, and Definitions

Terminology	*Acronym*	*Definition*
Principal Investigator	PI	Lead researcher on grant
Co-Principal Investigator	Co-PI	Support person for grant
Request for Proposal	RFP	Invitation to elicit grant proposal
Letter of Intent	LOI	Document indicating intention to submit grant application and proposal
Notice of Award	NOA	First formal indicator that grant has been awarded
Funder	F	The grant agency
Funding Opportunity Announcement	FOA	Funding description of grant
Not-for-Profit	NFP	Organization having not-for-profit status

a strong background or area of expertise in the topic related to the grant. This information is also provided in the form of supporting documentation to the funder such as the curriculum vitae (CV), publications, presentations, or any other prior funding and support.

Co-Principal Investigators (Co-PI). Sometimes simply listed as *co-principal investigators* (Co-PI), these are individuals who are supporting the development and implementation of a grant. While they are responsible for some aspect of the research, data collection, program implementation, or assessment, the Co-PIs do not typically have the authority to distribute or manage funds without the PI's discretion. There can sometimes be several Co-PIs on a grant, as allowed by each individual funder.

Letter of Intent (LOI). The *letter of intent* (LOI) is often the first step for many granting agencies. Preceding the call for applications or proposals, the letter of intent asks potential grantees to submit a one-page summary outlining the purpose of the grant/project, the need for funding, an estimated budget, any additional support, and ideas for assessment. The letter of intent is typically reviewed by a small panel, and then selected individuals are invited to submit a full grant proposal. The letter of intent is also sometime called the *letter of inquiry*.

Funding Opportunity Announcement (FOA). The *funding opportunity announcement* (FOA) is a description of funding made available for grant seekers. The FOA is primarily used by government agencies and is typically accompanied by a description and activity code.

Program Announcement (PA). In addition to the FOA, some government agencies (particularly National Institutes of Health [NIH]), release *program announcements* to denote important areas of funding. The PA highlights an area of increased priority, demonstrating a growing need and awareness in supporting research, projects, and programs that relate to the PA listed. Program announcements typically have longer, drawn-out deadlines that may be modified or updated after a few years. If a PA does not elicit strong proposals, it may be eliminated entirely.

Request for Proposals (RFP). Each granting agency announces that they have funding available with a *request for proposals* (RFP) announcement. Some agencies use different terminology, such as the National Institutes of Health, which asks for an RFA (request for applications). These proposals or applications outline the topic that is the theme or focus of the grant, the cycle (or timeline) for submission, review, and notification of acceptance or rejection, and the size of the funding available.

Notice of Award (NOA). While many different granting agencies have specific ways in which they inform grantees that a proposal was accepted or rejected, government agencies typically issue a *notice of award* (NOA) letter. This legal document is the official notification that an award is accepted and funds can be allocated for a project.

The Granting Agency (Funder). Any agency that has allocated funds for awarding grants is designated as the *granting agency*, or *funder*. This can be a government agency (e.g., National Science Foundation), a private funder (e.g., the Spencer Foundation), a local community funder (e.g., the Chicago Community Trust), a state funder (e.g., the Illinois Arts Council), or a funder available within a university (e.g., faculty development grants).

FFO—Federal Funding Opportunity. Most commonly associated with government grants, an FFO is another way for agencies to send out a request for proposals. This is traditionally presented as a federal funding opportunity, or can also be listed in more detail as a program announcement (PA).

501(c) 3—Not-for-Profit (NFP) Status. Many grants stipulate that funding will only be allocated to an organization that holds *not-for-profit status*. This is recognized by the United States Internal Revenue Code as being 501(c)3 for any institution that is exempt from federal income tax. Organizations such as universities and colleges fall under this category because their primary purpose is education. Many of these organizations' tax returns are available for review on the Internet.

Sustainability. The ability of an individual, organization, or institution to demonstrate that they are in strong fiscal health, will be able to successfully manage an award, and continue a research project or program even after funding commences is called *sustainability*. Sometimes, demonstrating sustainability is as simple as getting a letter of support from the university or a partnering institution.

These basic terms and definitions are the most commonly used and referenced within grant writing. However, every funding agency may have variations on these terms. Some agencies call an open application an RFP while others send out RFAs. Government agencies tend to use terms more synonymously than private foundations, who can release any RFP that meets their own needs. Familiarizing yourself with these general names will help when searching for grants and starting to write the proposal.

ETHICAL AND LEGAL CONSIDERATIONS

Grant writers need to understand some basic ethical and legal consideration involved with writing and administering grants. Most grants involve people, and often some degree of research, and you should always be concerned with protecting both the grant participants and grant team members. Nothing is worse in proposing or administering grants than to have harm come to the participants and experiencing a legal suit or formal complaint.

Any research or project that will be collecting data from human subjects requires the protection of human subjects in research. The NIH Office of Extramural Research provides one of the most widely disseminated training sessions for protecting human subject research participants. Many people mistakenly assume that even if the data they collect is "just for their own research" then they do not need to obtain informed consent from adults or assent forms for minors. In fact, this is one of the first steps to take prior to preparing and submitting a grant application.

Most institutions (e.g., colleges and universities) have an institutional research committee on human subjects, which is a body of internal professionals who reviews and approves any research-related project prior to the start of the research study. This committee is charged with ensuring that the proposed project conforms to institutional and professional standards in conducting research.

In many settings, the board that provides ethical, regulatory, and policy concerns regarding human subject research is the institutional review board (IRB Forum). The members of the scientific community participate in the IRB Forum in order to be involved with a community of researchers and support scholarly dialogue. This organization provides useful information and resources especially related to medical and scientific areas. For example, information on "informed consent" taken from the Code of

Federal Regulations Title XXI can typically be found on the IRB website (Tomal, 2010).

Several professional organizations (American Psychological Association and American Educational Research Association) have also provided guidelines on research and project ethics and protocol. Some of the ethical standards outlined by the American Psychological Association (APA) include obtaining an informed consent from the subjects, avoiding excessive financial inducements for participation, minimizing invasiveness (collection of information that could cause misconceptions or excessive risk to the subjects), and ensuring that participation in the project is voluntary.

Additionally, grant seekers need to demonstrate that they agree to share information with participants, agree not to deceive the participants, protect the subjects from harm (physical, emotional, and mental), and take reasonable measures to honor all commitments they have made to the participants. Being available for any questions or concerns through email or phone is also essential to protecting participant rights.

Keep in mind that most federal grant applications also include anti-discrimination regulations. For example, government grants need to comply with section 508 of the Rehabilitation Act of 1973 that prohibits discrimination against people with disabilities. Therefore, government assistance, using assistive technologies (e.g., screen readers), are provided to enable people with disabilities to access any information on the government grant sites. Grant seekers with disabilities are allowed by law to contact the government, explain the nature of their accessibility issues, and obtain assistance.

In addition, all people involved in grant writing or grant administration need to adhere to the laws and regulations of the Equal Employment Opportunity Commission (EEOC). The Origin Act prohibits discrimination on the basis of race, color, relation, national origin, and gender. This law covers most all aspects of employment and grant recipients and contractors.

The penalties associated with discrimination can be severe and have far-reaching consequences for your institution and for obtaining future grants.

In addition to the EEOC, violations of discrimination are also enforced and judgments can be awarded by state human rights commissions. For example, the State of Illinois has a Department of Human Rights Commission that is responsible for protecting individuals from discriminatory practices. Every state will be required to have a similar department. Assessments are generally made based upon the size of an organization and the severity of the action. Always consult your institution's legal counsel or grant agency for questions.

Finally, the American Grant Writers' Association (AGWA) and the Grant Professionals Association (GPA) are two of the nation's largest professional organizations and communities for grant writers, consultants, and educators. Each association lists specific criteria that they embrace and value as relevant and important when writing and administering grants. These criteria include complying with local and federal laws, effectively disclosing any conflicts of interest, and communicating in an appropriate manner with all granting agencies. Above all, there is an unspoken expectation that all awarded funds for any project will be allocated and used appropriately for the specific items listed within the original proposal.

GRANT MANAGEMENT SOFTWARE PROGRAMS

There are many grant management companies and programs that can assist you in locating funders, preparing proposals, and managing grants. Many of the software programs provide features such as application forms, sources of grants, matching applicants and grant capabilities, eligibility and pre-qualification assistance, report and grant management, budget support, and special grant database access.

Some grant software companies offer support groups, hardware, data, training, and online and personal grant consulting. Also, some of these companies provide community events for nonprofits including conferences, seminars, and workshops. Some software program names include Wizehive, Grants Network, Regpack, Fluid Review, Flexi-grants, Aims, Grant Manager, GranTracks, and Grants Cloud.

While it is not necessary to purchase or even use any of these programs, beginning grant writers often turn to grant management programs to assist them with the initial planning stages of their grant proposal. Considering how you will implement your project and manage the award you receive is a central component of creating a strong proposal. The funders want to see that not only are they supporting a worthwhile project, but that you can successfully carry out your goals once you receive the grant.

TAKING THE FIRST STEPS

The premise and purpose of this book is not to contend the right way to write a grant proposal, nor do we claim to have all the answers. Instead, the book is a response to the large number of resources available on "how to" write proposals, *get grants fast*!, or be successful in grant writing. The existing resources are often driven by the need to assist not-for-profits or community centers rather than focusing on the simple process of writing the grant. Much of the existing breadth of literature makes large claims suggesting that by following a formula or waving a magic wand, grants will suddenly appear.

Grant writing shares many similarities with research and scholarship, and because of that, the process of writing and getting grants is not necessarily something new. We hope that this book provides a general overview of grant writing for scholars and professionals, with outlines and ideas that can be easily applied to various disciplines. The book is meant to serve as a guide, to get back to the basics, to review the fundamentals of grant writing, management, and evaluation, so that you can write and apply for grants that can support your own ideas and projects.

This book is organized into six chapters and draws inferences from our love of music throughout. Chapter 1 was the overture to our symphony, presenting an overview of the grant writing field and hinting at some of the possibilities yet to come.

Chapter 2 delves deeper into the grant seeking process by exploring a funder's history and understanding the different types of granting agencies available. We discuss the process of finding different funding sources and identifying the differences amongst each type of granting agency. In essence, this is our exposition—our introduction into the themes of our grant writing proposal and the development of mutually beneficial and harmonious relationships with program officers.

In chapter 3, we uncover the theme and variations to our proposal as we shape the project statement and match needs with goals and outcomes. Your story and your voice should come through in the project statement as this is the heart of the grant proposal.

Chapter 4 presents the recapitulation, the process of completing the proposal by repeating our important themes as we weave the literature review, budget, and timeline together. This chapter incorporates the evaluation and assessment along with handy check lists that you can use to assess your grant proposals. It also includes examples of itemized budgets and narrative justifications.

Chapter 5 continues by examining the writing process as a finale, with ideas and examples for being concise, creative, and careful in your revisions and edits. Here, we discuss how you should not be afraid to restate your ideas throughout the proposal, making your points clear and familiar throughout the application. We also include examples of writing styles, strategies for writing succinctly, and active and passive styles of writing.

Finally, chapter 6 introduces the grant management process (if awarded), the next steps (if rejected), and the importance of forging collaborative relationships with colleagues, funders, and grants specialists. This is our encore—because it really is not over "until the fat lady sings." In the case of grant writing, a rejection only means opportunities for receiving feedback from program officers, revising proposals, and submitting the proposal again.

Scholars, professionals, students, independent researchers, consultants, and university faculty need support with grant writing. Unless you are fortunate to have a mentor, a senior faculty member, or a colleague who invites you into the grant writing world, you may be left alone. You will need to figure out and dissect the language, ideas, and process of grant writing.

The process can be overwhelming and intimidating, particularly if you did not have any prior experience, training, or background with how to pursue grants. Think back to your own educational experiences (perhaps both undergraduate and graduate); did you have any coursework that taught you how to write grants? Having attained doctorates from top-tier research institutions (an Ivy League university and a large Midwestern university, respectively), we can safely say, we did not. Our forays into grant writing emerged from a need to get grants, and a desire to support our own research and collaborative projects with external funding.

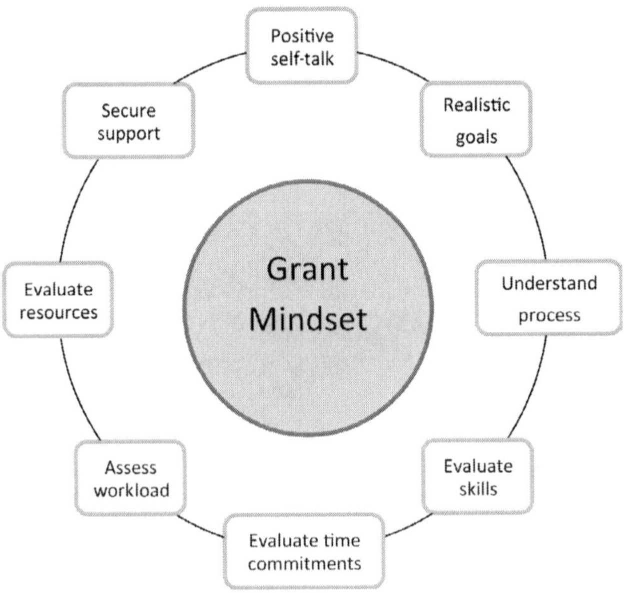

Figure 1.2. Developing a Grant Writing Mindset

What we have come to learn is that grant writing requires a certain mindset. In fact, it can often be equated with the ebbs and flows of being a professional musician. Figure 1.2 demonstrates the cyclical nature of grant writing and the steps that influence one another in this process. Assessing your own time, evaluating resources, setting realistic goals, and securing support are all components to being successful in grant writing. Sometimes, a simple pep talk or self-reassurance goes a long way.

Consider how many auditions, gigs, jobs, performances, or other types of musical experiences take place before one "hits it big." If some of the greatest musicians stopped after one rejection, we probably would have a much different trajectory of musical histories and genres.

While we have both been awarded a wide variety of grants (from small faculty development grants to larger collaborative projects), it is through trial and error, rejection and acceptance, that we came to recognize the *good* parts of grant writing (having a great idea), the *bad* parts of grant writing (another rejection), and realizing that through persistence, collaboration, and sometimes a little bit of luck, you are eventually awarded the *money*.

CHAPTER 1 NOTATIONS

1. Recognize that having a terminal degree does not equate having experience in grant writing.
2. Identify the components of a grant writing framework.
3. Familiarize yourself with the common terminology associated with grant writing.
4. Begin to develop a grant writing mindset.
5. Grant writing shares many facets with research and scholarship.

REFLECTION

If a funding agency approached you today and offered to fund any research project you wanted, what would you pursue? How would you begin to shape your ideas and support your own needs and vision with the goals of the funder? What might be some challenges?

2

Exposition

Finding the Grants

One of the many questions we are often asked by colleagues, researchers, and other grant seekers is "Where do you find grants?" The first place to begin is to understand the various resources available for applying for grants, and the funders who are willing to support our ideas, research, and projects. Begin by asking yourself this question: What is my field of study or project focus?

Narrowing down the specific discipline will help you focus on where to find grants and support. For example, a project that focuses on arts integration within public schools in New York City is not going to have any viable funding options from the National Institutes of Health. Similarly, a research study that looks at the impact of gene-environment interactions on cognitive decline within a large, homogenous population would most likely be appealing to a group like the Alzheimer's Association of America. In fact, it was funded for a research project by National Institutes of Health in 2014.

Additionally, it is important to recognize that every funding agency has different expectations and requirements. No two funders will fund the same project. Some funders will only fund the same research while others will never fund the same ideas twice. The National Institutes of Health has different priorities than the National Science Foundation or the National Endowment for the Arts.

These priorities will also change with the need of the community and the focus of the funder. An RFP that was open for many years might close indefinitely if the funder believes that it was not serving any reciprocal focus or making an impact on the funder's overarching goals.

Table 2.1. Grant Agencies and Programs

Grant Agencies	*Sample Programs*
Government	National Institutes of Health, National Endowment for the Humanities, National Science Foundation, National Endowment for the Arts
Private Foundations	Grammy Foundation, Alzheimer's Association, Bill and Melinda Gates Foundation, Spencer Foundation, Whitehall Foundation, American Psychological Association
Corporate Foundations	Toyota Foundation, PepsiCo, Best Buy Foundation, Ford Foundation

So how, then, does anyone without specific grants training, expertise, or experience with grants begin to even apply for a grant? There are many general categories of grants available for supporting the goals of individuals, small organizations, or collaborations between a researcher and a not-for-profit. These typically include grants provided by the government, foundations and corporations, fellowships, and institutional grant sources. Table 2.1 categorizes several funding opportunities by government, private, and corporate agencies. This is not a comprehensive list but meant to serve as an example of what funding is available at the national level.

GOVERNMENT GRANTS

Some of the largest funding resources available come from government agencies. However, the amount of funding available by discipline largely varies. Consider that for the FY2015, the United States allocated nearly $150 million for the National Endowment for the Arts, $7 billion for the National Science Foundation, $69 billion for the Education Department, and $300 billion for the National Institute of Health (White House Budget, 2015.

These large variances in funding represent not only the priorities of the government, but the need and value that is placed on these areas of research. So, an individual applying for a large arts-research grant will likely be asking for around $50,000, while a large research grant in medicine might allocate nearly $4 million for a multi-year project.

Government grants also have very specific guidelines for awards and in reporting findings. This is partly attributed to the fact that government agencies are "public organizations spending public monies" (Sokolow,

2009, p. 1). There are often specific expectations on how data should be collected, what percentage of the data should be quantitative, and how the funds can be applied. Consider that a grant from the United States Department of Education requires at least 80 percent of the assessment data collected during the grant to be quantitative.

While government granting agencies are willing to fund individual, scholarly research, they also look for collaborative efforts, such as between multiple principal investigators, or projects that will impact a large community. Most people think of government grants as coming from large funding agencies such as the National Science Foundation or the National Endowment for the Humanities. However, the importance of community in government funding is apparent in local branches of these national agencies.

For example, while the National Endowment for the Arts might request a large sum of money from the United States Fiscal Budget, local agencies in each state (such as the Illinois Arts Council) can make requests to the National Endowment for the Arts for funds to support smaller, local projects. The local agencies can then provide support to individual researchers, small not-for-profits, or other community-based organizations. This, in turn, creates a tiered effect of how funds are distributed.

Government grants also have a laborious application process. A majority of government grants have been consolidated within Grants.gov for application and submission. The Grants.gov submission requires several steps including being set up with the System for Award Management (SAM), a one-time registration on eRA Commons, and being ready to submit an SF-424 at least six weeks in advance of the actual application deadline.

For example, the National Endowment for the Arts requires an SF-424 be submitted at least one month prior to beginning the proposal for a grant. Once the SF-424 is submitted, you will receive a tracking number for your grant, which will then allow you to open your application and submit your materials. This essentially means that you are starting the application process nearly two to three months before the deadline.

In addition to supplying the basic financial information for your organization or center, government grants often require supplementary documents such as letters of support. These letters can indicate research support (such as access to private datasets), fiscal support (demonstrating sustainability from your institution), or support from another organization. Letters of support are important in demonstrating the success and viability of your project. Funders are more likely to give you an award if they feel you will be successful in implementing your project and continuing your research even after the award is over.

Additional supplementary documents may include your resume or CV, reference lists, detailed information on personnel involved, evidence of training in the protection of human subjects research, examples of instruments that will be used in data collection (for primary data analysis), or documents stating access to data (for secondary data analysis). It is not unusual for a government grant application to exceed 100 pages.

All of these materials should be uploaded with your application. Importantly, one of the best recommendations we can make is to have your application materials (proposal, budget, timeline, personnel, evaluation) written out prior to even opening the application on Grants.gov. If you are prepared in advance, the actually applying becomes a simple process of copying and pasting information.

FOUNDATION GRANTS

When we think of grants coming from private foundations, we often equate these awards with celebrity. Think of some of the top foundations in the United States—Bill and Melinda Gates Foundation, Spencer Foundation, and Grammy Foundation. Foundation grants vary in their availability for organizations and individuals. While some have historically provided grants for both categories of grant seekers, the majority of foundation grants are awarded to organizations.

A priority for foundations is also organizations that work within specific communities and target a need within a designated population. For example, the Ford Foundation clearly distinguishes grants for organizations and individuals on its website. However, when selecting "individuals" as an option there is a large disclaimer that grants are primarily given to organizations. The foundation also requests that inquiries be made using their predesigned template to avoid large number of queries being directed to individual program officers.

Smaller, local foundation grants are also associated with being family foundations, that is, private funding established through families who are interested in philanthropy or simply want to establish a fund in a family member's name. These foundations are often very specific in what they will fund, often focusing on a particular discipline or field of study that is particularly relevant to their own family's mission.

Perhaps the greatest difference between government grants and foundation grants is the accessibility and flexibility of the funders. While government grants are known for being rigid about deadlines and details, foundations tend to be more fluid with applications, contact with program officers, or simply awarding funding. Even if you feel a program does not necessarily fit with a foundation's RFP, reaching out to a program officer or providing additional information to support your project idea may make all the difference in funding.

It is important that when applying to any family foundation that you familiarize yourself with that foundation's goals and objectives. Many foundations are very specific in terms of what they will fund, their expectations for the writing tone, and the programs they will support. It is always a good idea to reach out to a program officer. In some cases, the foundation would request that you establish a meeting prior to even applying for funding. For instance, some family foundations that support artistic endeavors require actually seeing a performance or exhibition prior to even receiving a funding application.

Similar to any type of granting agency, foundations are trying to further their own missions and ideals. Unlike government grants that are furthered by policies or federal agendas, private foundations can create their own vision for providing grants. Therefore, in addition to familiarizing yourself with the foundation's mission, understanding the local community, needs, and demographics that surround the foundation you are contacting will help you further augment your chances of receiving an award.

FELLOWSHIPS AND SCHOLARSHIPS

Perhaps most widely equated with academia are fellowships and scholarships—awards that are given based on merit, potential for contribution to the field, and importance of research. Fellowships are available from both government agencies and private funders and vary in their award amounts, duration, and requirements. Unlike the majority of grants geared toward collaborative projects, fellowships and scholarships are primarily awarded to individuals.

Being awarded a fellowship is often a highlight of a scholar's career, cementing one's research in the literature, and demonstrating value for individual research. Grants awarded by the United States Department of Education, the National Science Foundation Graduate Research Fellowship Program, or the Dissertation Completion Fellowship from the American Council of Learned Societies (ACLS) support early scholars during their studies, assisting them in completing their graduate education.

The Fulbright Scholars Program is one of the most widely recognized and respected fellowship programs in the United States, bringing together scholars from a variety of disciplines to collaborate with colleagues in international educational institutions. Similarly, the Guggenheim Fellowship is one of the highest awards of artistic merit, given only to those scholars who have made a strong impact in the arts. Other programs such as the MacArthur Foundation Fellowship do not accept unsolicited nominations or applications and have their own steering committee for recommending potential fellows.

While fellowships definitely bring with them a certain level of prestige and honor, their narrow focus and specific eligibility requirements make it challenging to apply. Fellowships typically expect their applicants to have some strong background, education, training, or experience in their discipline.

CORPORATE GRANTS

If private foundations have a large, philanthropic mission, then they often are magnified by corporate funders. Large corporations are very focused on what their mission is and how their grants will impact their own image. Consider that the Foundation Center has listed the Wells Fargo Foundation, Bank of America Foundation, Ford Foundation, and Citi Foundation in their top ten largest corporate funders by the amount that they donated (Foundation Center, 2014).

The majority of these projects, however, are not awarded to individual faculty conducting academic research. Rather, the funds are distributed to projects that focus on community development, environmental stewardship, or sustainability of energy-efficient resources. Let us consider the Best Buy Foundation as an example. The foundation is an extension of the Best Buy electronic stores across the United States. Their focus is on projects that merge communities, schools, teenagers, and technology.

While the focus of the Best Buy Foundation may seem general and appealing for those working in secondary school settings, further reading of their eligibility guidelines indicates a priority for projects that are willing to integrate their "Geek Squad Academy" into the curriculum, or collaborate with the "Teen Tech" centers they have designated as target sites across the country.

Corporate grants are just that—awards being distributed by large corporations. Above all else, the funds they distribute are driven almost entirely by their own mission. Additionally, consider that many corporate grants are somehow affiliated with the largest banks in the nation. This is another way corporations maintain their own sustainability in building and supporting grant applications.

It should be acknowledged that while giving is inherently a part of philanthropy, it also supports and promotes an image that is important to the funder. Corporate grants are often large amounts of funding provided to support projects that demonstrate sustainability. The mission of large corporations is often to demonstrate how they impact humanity and human life, and many of these awards are given to programs that collaborate with communities in international settings.

STARTING SMALL

While reaching for the largest grant is often the most appealing prospect in grant writing, sometimes it is better to start small, and apply for more accessible local grants. Smaller, community-based grants are often available through various local organizations that are willing to fund specific research projects or are looking for partnerships with universities or colleges in the area.

Consider the following example. Rather than applying for a grant to support arts education research from the National Endowment for the Arts (an award that is notoriously difficult for an individual research scholar to receive anyway), applying for a smaller grant through the Illinois Arts Council or the Chicago Community Trust would be a more realistic approach when looking for funding.

As mentioned earlier, smaller, local foundations are often already supported with grants from larger funding agencies. The Illinois Arts Council typically applies for and receives funding from the National Endowment for the Arts (NEA). Furthermore, every state is mandated to have a division of cultural affairs. In this role, the director is responsible for seeking and managing grants at the federal and state level and can be a great resource for supporting the grant process. A grant application submitted to the NEA by an individual scholar would then be competing against a larger research proposal submitted by the Illinois Arts Council.

Starting with smaller grants can also give you an advantage when applying for larger funds. When a national or government organization sees that you have been awarded a smaller grant, they may be more willing to take risks and support your research, acknowledging that another foundation or funding agency has already invested themselves in your work.

MAKING SENSE OF THE MISSION STATEMENT

While these descriptions of different funding agencies are broad, general definitions, understanding where potential funders have priorities will help you plan your individual or collaborative projects. Figure 2.1 outlines the different funding agencies and their funding priorities as described in this chapter. The column for collaborative projects indicates that funders expect a partnership between at least two different institutions.

Grant Sources	Individual Research	501(c)3 Not-for-Profits	Collaborative Projects
Government		X	X
Foundations		X	X
Corporations		X	X
Fellowships	X		
Institutional	X		X

Figure 2.1. Examples of Grant Agencies and Funding Priorities

Each funder, regardless of the purpose or funding priority, strives to fulfill a declared mission. This mission then informs what projects are funded, the locations and communities receiving funding, and the individuals whose research will, in turn, represent the granting agency. Understanding a funder's mission will help you identify if a granting agency is a good fit for your work.

A funder is also more likely to support a project that aligns with its own mission. For example, the National Endowment for the Humanities clearly states that the grants are awarded to universities, libraries, museums, or independent scholars. Furthermore, the grants should "strengthen teaching and learning in schools and colleges, and facilitate research and original scholarship" amongst other components of their mission (NEH, 2014).

This idea has already been reiterated in the application process for government, private foundations, and corporate grants, but its value cannot be overstated. The mission of a funder is what drives all awards. Therefore, if your proposal does not match the mission statement or align with what a funder presents as being important to them, your chance of securing funding is greatly diminished. If there is any confusion about the vision, mission, or focus of a funder, reaching out to a program officer is always the best option.

LOOKING BACK TO GO FORWARD

Once you have selected some potential funders who might support your project, search within the agencies' different funding priorities, RFPs, and deadlines, and create a list of potential applications. For example, the

National Institutes of Health has several different branches of research and specializations, and within those sections are different grant opportunities. A scholar seeking funding for a large, multi-year research project would probably apply for an R01 research grant within a specific department and field.

Often times, determining whether a funder is a good match for a project is one of the initial challenges. After creating a list of potential funders for your own research and projects, begin by searching through the funder's award *history*. This information is typically grouped under sections titled past awards, previous grants, or awards by year. Reading through these lists will give you a strong idea of (1) what types of projects the funder is interested in supporting, and (2) which individuals, fields, disciplines, or organizations they tend to primarily support.

Think of this step in the grant writing process as looking back—that is, looking through a funder's past to understand where they will give awards in the future. As an example, a colleague was once interested in submitting a grant to develop music education curriculum to the Grammy Foundation. However, upon researching the foundation's funding history it became apparent that the majority of grants were awarded to hospitals or universities investigating the link between musical learning and playing with the functions of the brain.

In addition to reviewing the funder's history, note the different organizations, universities, communities, or individuals that have received awards from this granting agency. This is because a funder is more likely to support projects with similar goals and outcomes. During a grant workshop, one of our colleagues asked where to look for grants to support the university's center for social justice, teaching, and learning. One of our suggestions included looking at similar centers across the state (and nation) and locating where they were receiving funding.

DEADLINES AND DILEMMAS

Every granting agency has a deadline for when the application is due. These deadlines are essentially untenable because of the number of applications that a funder may receive and the time it takes to send applications out for a peer-review process. Rarely do funders allow for late submissions or extensions when applying for grants, so noting down deadlines is as important as finding the funding source.

Some people take years to write and submit a grant while others can pull together a proposal in a few weeks. Regardless of how long it takes you to write the proposal, you should allocate at least two weeks to work on the online submission of a grant application. If you wait until the day of the deadline there is too great of a risk of missing the submission because of external factors related to errant technology, familial issues, or neglecting to submit the application.

Grants.gov recommends allocating at least five days for *submitting* grants for federal funds. We recommend at least ten days for the submission process. The online submission portal in Grants.gov has numerous specifications and requirements for submitting a completed grant application. Some of these processes include confirming your eligibility to apply for a grant, getting registered with Grants.gov, and familiarizing yourself with the various forms and resources on the website. These steps are *in addition to* the grant proposal itself, which can be nearly 100 pages in length.

Government agencies will also have specific log-in information for your personal account and a separate log-in number for each grant application that you begin. It is important to track each of these accounts as separate so that any follow-up questions or revisions are appropriately connected with the correct application. This becomes even more necessary as you start multiple applications for different RFPs.

Some funders also have rolling deadlines, which means that applications will be considered as they are submitted, or accept grant proposals on a quarterly basis. However, these types of deadlines are rare and are often limited to funding from private foundations or fellowships. Typically, a funder will have two or three major deadlines, within which there can be one or several RFPs. If there is any question as to the deadline for an application, it is best to email or call the program officer connected with the grant program.

The majority of funders also provide grant seekers with the opportunity to receive information on when an RFP will be released, or when new grants become available. This information is invaluable! Even if you may forget about a potential funder, they will email you to remind you about an open application.

When accessing a funder's website, there is usually a link to submit your email address to receive updated information on grants and applications. Although it may seem time-consuming to find each funder's link and individually request information on grants, taking the time to submit your email will save you time in the future, and allow you to be directly notified when a grant application submission period begins.

Grants are also organized by the length of time that funding is available. For example, the NIH offers an R01 and an R21. Individuals who have experience applying for an NIH grant will immediately be able to identify that an R01 is a larger, multi-year grant program, while an R21 typically funds pilot projects or smaller interventions. In fact, many people who are eventually awarded a prestigious R01 grant have successfully received an R21 focusing on a similar topic.

While smaller grants can be one-time awards, for a few months, larger grants can be renewed or extended for several years. Consider that grant-funded medical research is often supported for many years, sometimes spanning decades, as longitudinal projects track the changes or outcomes of clinical trials in patients.

Contrastingly, funding for an intervention program or professional development for teachers might be a single award that could be applied within a twelve-month period. Funds distributed to community centers, arts programs, or school-based projects are typically granted for up to one year. This is also so funders can determine the viability and sustainability of your research or project, and assess whether it is something they may be interested in supporting again in the future.

As you plan your proposal, identify how long you may need funding for your project. If you are implementing a pilot program, a smaller funding agency may be able to provide immediate support. If you have already established an idea and documented initial success or innovation in your own field, applying for a larger, renewable grant may allow you to further explore your research.

Regardless of the deadline approaching, your intent for applying should begin well in advance of a call for proposals. If you realize that a deadline is approaching or you missed one altogether, use that as an opportunity to be prepared for the next cycle. In fact, any experienced grant writer will recommend that you apply for a later deadline rather than trying to crunch numbers at the last minute.

THE LETTER OF INTENT

Many funders, especially those that receive thousands of grant applications, do not have time to read through lengthy, dense proposals. Therefore, a small review panel will be asked to select and invite potential applicants from a pool of grant seekers who submit a letter of intent or inquiry. The *letter of intent* is a summary of your project, objectives, budget, and evaluation.

Do you recall the first time you wrote a cover letter to a potential employer? You probably succinctly summarized your work, goals, and ideas within one page. You tried your best to be enthusiastic, persuasive, honest, and intriguing. These are the same qualities that should encompass your letter of inquiry. A strong letter of inquiry or intent typically includes five points:

1. The project title and statement
2. Summary of the objectives of the project

3. Methodology for data collection and assessment
4. Budget and timeline
5. Individuals involved with the grant

The letter of intent is essentially the selling point—you are marketing your idea to the highest bidder. Make sure you have an interesting title for your grant. The title is the first thing reviewers are going to read. It should instantly tell a reviewer what your grant is about and why it is important.

If someone asked you to review LOIs and you read through hundreds of proposals, what would stand out to you? What key elements in the project, ideas, writing style, or outcomes would you find interesting? Putting yourself in the perspective of the granting agency may help you find ways to make your own LOI unique.

Being a good grant writer involves not only being able to demonstrate brevity with your ideas, but the ability to be persuasive at the same time. In one or two pages, you are essentially convincing someone to select your proposal, to invite you to submit a full application, to find your work more interesting and important than someone else's ideas.

For example, when submitting a letter of inquiry to the Ford Foundation, you are limited to 100 words for the purpose of the project, and another 100 words for the problems and issues the project will address. Exceeding the required page limit may cost you points or prevent you from entering additional information in their online application.

After spending hours writing a proposal and adding as many details as possible, we hope that our applications are read by the reviewers and given due consideration. The reality, however, is that many times the proposals are then edited down by program officers so that the executive board reads and reviews just one page. Even if you are not required to write a LOI, sometimes starting your proposal with one will help you outline your key ideas and summarize your work.

MAKING A CALL

As you continue your search for potential funders, remember that just as you are trying to find a funder for your project, someone is trying to find a project that they deem worthy to fund. This is what we will continue to describe as the reciprocal process of funding. Any granting agency—public or private—has designated funds to support projects. Ensuring that the project is a good fit is a reciprocal process. You have to shape the grant proposal to be relevant to the funder, and the funder reviews the proposal to ensure that it aligns with its own goals and mission.

Every granting agency also has program managers (or program officers) who are assigned to different grants, projects, or programs. For example, when the United States Department of Education released an RFP for a new grant to support research in higher education, a project manager was listed along with the RFP. In addition to her name, the USDE provided the project manager's email and phone number. This individual is then solely responsible for answering any queries related to the RFP, organizing and managing incoming proposals, and contacting awarded and rejected projects. In essence, this program manager is your "go-to gal."

With the amount of time we spend checking our emails, typing, texting, and tweeting, think about how often we take the time to pick up the phone to talk, ask questions, or simply hold a conversation. Grant writing is not just a process, it is a partnership, one that relies heavily on collaboration within the grant proposal, in the granting institution, and with the program officers at the funding agency.

Building a meaningful relationship with the program manager is an important place to start. Consider it as a reciprocal relationship, one in which both parties should be mutually beneficial and harmonious. This does not mean that you will get "the upper-hand" when applying for a grant, rather it is akin to developing any professional relationship with colleagues.

This becomes particularly relevant once you submit the grant. The program manager becomes a contact person for assisting with managing a grant, or providing feedback if a proposal is rejected. In fact, many scholars have built relationships with program managers for decades. Figure 2.2 outlines some of the initial steps in the grant writing process, starting with finding a granting agency to contacting the officer before applying.

Fostering these relationships proves to be invaluable in the grant writing process, particularly when acknowledging that some agencies do not use blinded peer reviews. Developing lifelong partnerships with program managers is as important to establishing a grant writing agenda as building relationships with colleagues at your own universities and institutions. This demonstrates a mutual understanding of the time and commitment it takes to write and manage grants. Remember that a program manager may be reading through and receiving hundreds of applications a day.

Some of the best ways to develop and maintain relationships with program managers is through the process called *soft touches*. A soft touch is any action that you take to stay in contact with the program manager. Some of these include sending email updates, initiating periodic phone calls, sending an e-news letter, mailing or emailing personal notes, and sending articles of interest.

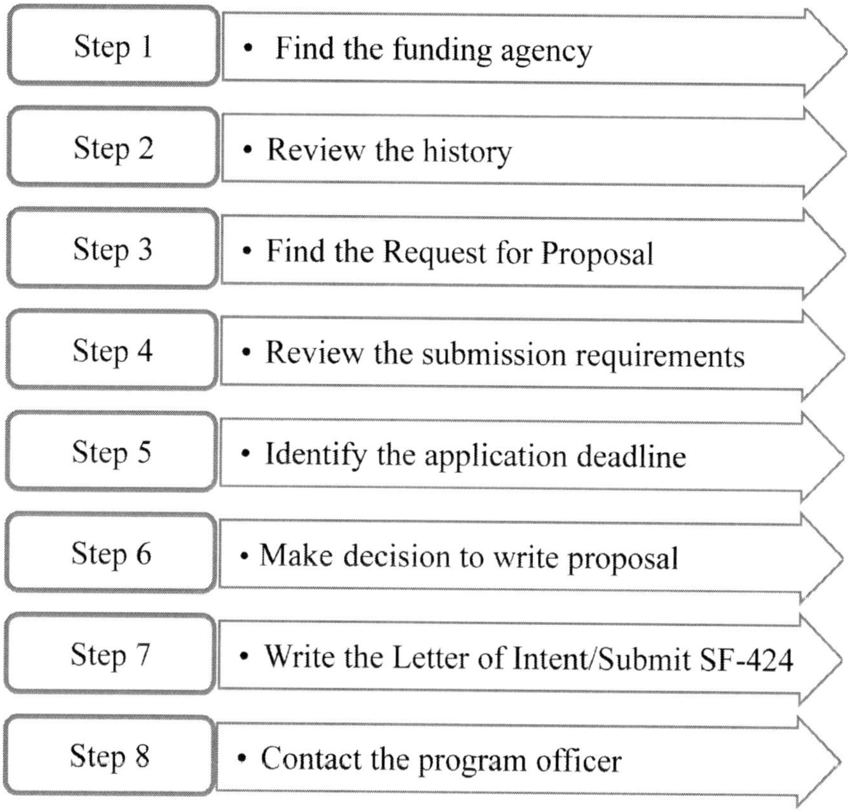

Figure 2.2. Initial Steps in Grant Writing

You should also recognize that you may never know when you might meet a potential program manager. So, you need to ready for the encounter by always having your business card and your *elevator talking points.* The elevator talking points concept implies that you have thirty seconds to ride the elevator and make your pitch to someone of influence. So, you need to rehearse your lines succinctly to make the best impression you can. During this time you might ask about upcoming grants, your interests, status of application reviews, and future agency funding outlooks.

Importantly, if you want to reach out to a program manager, have a face-to-face meeting, or simply discuss potential granting opportunities, do not hesitate to set up a meeting. Program managers are there to help with the grant writing and awarding processes. Their job is to ensure that a granting agency provides funds to the applications of greatest quality and need. Program managers are interested and willing to assist you in the submission process.

The process of finding the grants is really the beginning of establishing a grant writing agenda. Attending one-day seminars or workshops related to grant writing may seem appealing, but many times the organizers are pitching their own expertise and charging expensive fees without providing avenues for applying knowledge. Be cautious of websites or programs that charge excessive amounts of money for assistance with grant submissions. You should not have to pay money to submit a grant application. However, working with a professional grant writer as a consultant may help you as you begin the process.

Find places to network with other professionals (i.e., national conferences in your field), where grant writing is a part of the natural conversation. Many people imagine that they will eventually write a grant but getting started is the challenge. Connecting with someone who may have prior experience or working with a colleague to write a grant together for the first time can prove to be an invaluable learning opportunity. This will also strengthen your ideas of what is currently being funded within your discipline as you continue to foster collaborative relationships.

CHAPTER 2 NOTATIONS

1. Look to the funder's past to understand where they will fund in the future.
2. Find similar research at other centers, organizations, or institutions, and see who funded their projects.
3. Do not dismiss a deadline—make note of when the RFP was announced and when the grant submission is due.
4. Summarize the project's goals, outcomes, budget, timeline, and personnel for an LOI.
5. Do not be afraid to pick up the phone and talk with the program manager.

REFLECTION

There are many different sources for pursuing grants. What are some of the differences between public and private funders? Which organizations are more likely to align their own funding priorities with your own project ideas? What are the challenges of applying for government grants versus foundations?

3

Theme and Variations

Developing the Proposal

After finding the funder, locating an RFP, and contacting the program manager, the actual grant writing begins. To many people, this is the easy part. As scholars, researchers, independent consultants, or just passionate individuals, we have many ideas, projects, collaborations, or just brainstorms of potential research. We spend hours collecting literature, pulling different threads together to create a framework, finding the statement that defines our project, and outlining the questions we will explore and the data we will gather.

Grant writing is the same process. In many ways, grant writing is a close relative to scholarly research, perhaps realized as the younger siblings, tagging along behind, a constant reminder that they are there, and need attention, even though you just do not have the time.

Consider how in an orchestral symphony we are introduced to the theme, the motifs, and the opening ideas presented to us by the composer. These themes are then repeated, manipulated, and referenced throughout the musical score, reminding us of their purpose and presence. Similarly, the process of writing the proposal and shaping your ideas is your variations on the themes you have already decided. By now, you have selected potential funders and programs that are requesting proposals. The next steps are pulling everything together.

Similar to writing a paper or scholarly article, grant proposals have specific components that comprise the narrative section of an application. Narratives are the heart of a grant proposal—they tell your story, the purpose of the project, and the need for funding support. While funders may vary in the specific requirements that are outlined for the narrative, the majority of grant proposals ask for the following six components:

1. Executive Summary
2. The Project Statement
3. Purpose and Rationale
4. Goals and Outcomes
5. Assessment
6. Personnel

These different components collectively outline the entire grant proposal. There may be specific terms, subheadings, or requirements within each application. Following the grant applications outline is extremely important. However, funders may not always use the same language in their applications.

In some instances, the project statement, purpose, and rationale may fall under a category of "major project activities" without any specific area for including a literature review or references. Additionally, the evaluation or assessment might be required as a supplementary document. Review the outline of each grant application before beginning to organize your narrative.

THE EXECUTIVE SUMMARY

The executive summary is often what is shared with the board when final granting decisions are made—so as you begin to write the proposal and develop your ideas, continue to think about how to summarize key points into one page. The executive summary also highlights what is important or unique about your project, what key findings have already developed within this research area, or paths that you wish to further explore.

If you do include an executive summary, remember that you are using this section of the proposal to capture your audience's attention, to grab your reader, and make a good first impression. Consider some of the main points of your grant proposal. What do you hope to accomplish? What makes your proposal innovative? What makes your ideas unique?

The executive summary can also be modified from an existing letter of intent. The LOI is often structured in a similar format, as quick introduction to what it is you hope to do and how you will accomplish your goals. Make your statements compelling and choose your words carefully. Sometimes, people will not read past the executive summary and will decide what proposals to further review based on this initial reading.

THE PROJECT STATEMENT

As you begin work on your project statement, you may find yourself asking, *am I writing a research paper or a grant proposal?* When, in fact, the two are very much alike. The project statement is telling the funder what is the overall focus of the grant application. It explains the goals and outcomes, the need for funding to support your idea, and the impact of your research on the community.

Writing a grant proposal is all about persuasion. You must persuade the funder to select your proposal over another. Remember Aristotle's famous Greek terms for persuasion—ethos (be credible), pathos (be passionate), and logos (be factual). Consider also the basics of writing a persuasive paragraph. Include facts, cite credible sources, provide examples, and address any opposing viewpoints.

Some of the key ways to convince your reader is by starting out with strong facts. Include some descriptive statistics in your opening statement to draw in your reader. For example, when applying for a grant through the National Institute on Aging (NIA), an opening statement could read as follows:

> Older adults comprise 13 percent of the population in the United States; research on their daily living, social and cognitive functioning, as well as healthy aging has been of considerable interest to researchers.

This statement immediately tells the reader that the grant proposal will work with a sample of older adults, and further compounds that this population is important because (a) they comprise a strong percentage of the population, and (b) researchers are interested in understanding the aging process.

When including any descriptive statistics (e.g., addressing the population of your study or project), make sure to cite credible sources. There are many scholarly articles and journals that provide examples of prior research, but you could also use government databases, newspaper articles, or information from multimedia sources. Check to see if the granting agency requires references and if they use a particular reference style.

After you have established the opening statements and drawn your reader into the purpose of your project, consider giving some examples of what has currently been *done* and what you plan to *do* if you are awarded the grant. Let us build on the statement regarding older adults:

> Older adults comprise 13 percent of the population in the United States; research on their daily living, social and cognitive functioning, as well as healthy aging has been of considerable interest to researchers. *In fact, the*

> *National Endowment for the Arts (NEA) convened a task force to outline the challenges faced with exploring the impact of the arts on the health and well-being of older adults.*

With the addition of this next sentence, we are referencing a government agency, and demonstrating a national interest and agenda in funding projects that support and explore the aging process.

To build on this project statement, consider what ideas could expand what is already being done. After establishing what currently exists, the next step is to state what your project will do and how it addresses the needs of your field or discipline. The opening statement (without references and additional statistical data) could then look like this:

> Older adults comprise 13 percent of the population in the United States; research on their daily living, social and cognitive functioning, as well as healthy aging has been of considerable interest to researchers. In fact, the National Endowment for the Arts (NEA) convened a task force to outline the challenges faced with exploring the impact of the arts on the health and well-being of older adults.
>
> *While the focus of research on the role music plays in cognitive reserve and control has primarily centered on investigations in musical training and music making, a lesser investigated phenomenon is the impact of passive arts participation on cognitive function.*

Here, we are telling the reviewers what is missing and what needs to be done. This step in the development of the project statement is very similar to writing the problem and purpose statement of a thesis or dissertation. You are essentially showing the need for your project and why it should be funded.

Your next steps would be to provide supporting statements (through citations) to demonstrate the need for your research or project. You should list the major activities that will take place. Sometimes, the list comes in the form of a bulleted outline, while other times it makes more sense to continue the flow of the application with a narrative description. That decision is again based on the requirements of the application.

FINDING YOUR VOICE

The project statement is very much the essence and the heart of the grant proposal. You are telling your story, voice, and perspective. Many funders and program managers have stated that when reading through proposals, they look for the story and search for the passion in the narrative. Essentially, you are convincing someone to invest in your work and your ideas by giving a strong rationale for your need for funding. The objective is to persuade a funder to believe in your proposal and choose your project over someone else's application.

Your ideas should move as a melodic line in music, hinting at the themes you introduce in the project statement throughout your entire proposal. You are constantly telling and reminding the audience of the importance of your work. As you write and revise the project statement continue to ask yourself, *what is my story?*

Funders want to know what type of change or impact will be made with your project. They are interested in knowing the potential outcomes and how this research will contribute to the existing body of literature and how this project will impact their own goals. In fact, one of the main criteria often used in determining whether a proposal will receive funding or not is whether the goals outlined in the project statement match their own goals.

Consider answering the following questions: *Who will be involved with the grant? What do we want to accomplish?* And *How will funding be used?* These questions will help shape the overall focus of your proposal and demonstrate the need for the award. Try to keep a persuasive but concise tone in your writing—remember that you are competing with others for a similar grant. Make your voice unique.

Very rarely do funders award a grant without asking for anything in return (with the exception of an award such as the MacArthur Fellowship). And, in these instances, awards are made based on recommendations from an external panel, rather than through solicited requests for proposals.

PURPOSE AND RATIONALE

A good project statement should have both detail and brevity. Reviewers typically score grant proposals with rubrics or rating scales that evaluate how well a project statement is written and the value of this project in relation to the funder's own mission and goals. Let us evaluate the following project statement as an example using the project statement evaluation chart:

> The purpose of this grant is to support the development of an arts education program that serves students in K–6 elementary schools as they learn about dance and literacy.

Write down three ways that you might change this statement—how can it be better? What needs more focus, clarification, or support? What would you be looking for if you were the potential funder?

First, this project statement is contradictory. It begins by referencing the development of a program but then continues to say that it already serves students in an elementary setting. Reviewers will not know whether the project has already begun or whether funding is needed to develop the program. Is the grant going to support the development (meaning the projects has not begun), or is it supporting a program that already exists and "serves" students in the school? Something as simple as subject-verb agreement and verb tense can influence your grant proposal.

Second, unless the program, grant, or project has already established a strong partnership with a school, it is extremely difficult to begin a new program for students across kindergarten through sixth grade. This is a huge age range! The ways in which kindergartners learn is very different from how sixth-graders learn. Be specific in your goals and outcomes. Will the program address the needs of early elementary students or upper elementary? How many students will participate? How many schools? How many classrooms?

The more specific information you can provide, the more a grant reviewer will understand your proposal. It will also demonstrate that you have done work prior to applying for the grant. Focusing on one or two grade levels shows potential funders that your idea is realistic and attainable.

Third, a program that teaches students about dance and literacy is extremely broad in scope. What is the purpose of the program? A dance teacher will ask, what are students learning in dance, while a classroom teacher will ask, what are students learning through literacy. If you are unsure of what exactly could be accomplished, enlist the help of a dance teacher and a classroom teacher. Invite them to be a part of the application process so that their expertise is evident in the examples you provide.

A stronger statement would be to write that *students will develop phonemic awareness through creative movement*, or *use their bodies to make the different letters in the alphabet*. Now, the statements are clear, measurable, and precise. Someone who does not have any background or understanding of dance or literacy can still understand what it is you hope to accomplish. This gives funders an idea of *what* the program is going to do and *how* the goals will be achieved.

Let us examine a different version of this project statement, one that has begun to expand on these basic ideas:

> A small interdisciplinary arts organization wants to find funding for a new project that will engage teaching artists in collaboration with kindergarten teachers. The idea is to find ways to support students' reading fluency and emergent reading skills by teaching lessons through music composition. The organization has $10,000 of funding to help start this program but needs at

> least $15,000 to build a partnership for two years. There are a total of four teaching artists and two elementary schools that will be involved with the project.

While this statement gives more details and examples of the focus of the project, the innovative idea, and the potential collaborations between an organization, school, teachers, and artists, there are still many components that would be unclear or confusing for potential funders.

One of the first ways to revise this statement is to consider the audience reading the proposal. Be conscious of the language you use in your project statement. A potential reviewer may not know what emergent reading skills are and will, therefore, be confused with what you are trying to do. If you are using language specific to a field or discipline, consider including definitions in the proposal to situate your idea within a given context.

Additionally, the statement mentions how much money the organization has but it is unclear whether the program needs $5,000 more (to have a total of $15,000) or $15,000 more (to have a total of $25,000) to build and sustain a partnership. If you are breaking down examples of the budget in the project statement, make sure you specify how much you have, how much is needed, and how much you are seeking.

Finally, much more information is needed to understand the scope and sequence of this project. What will the teaching artists and teachers be *doing*? How are the students *learning* about dance and literacy? How will you *use* the funds to support professional development, student activities, and assessment over this two-year period of time?

Notice the italicized words in the previous paragraph. These words—doing, learning, and use—are all verbs that denote an action being taken. Including strong action words in your project statement will reinforce the ideas that the funds will be allocated to implement a project. This is not just an idea, but one that you have planned and can successfully accomplish.

Remember, a funder can sometimes receive hundreds of applications for a grant, and reviewers are looking for what makes a grant unique and stand out from the others. In a short amount of time, reviewers need to understand *what* you propose to do with their money and *how* you plan to be successful. With that in mind, the project statement essentially summarizes why *you* should be the one getting the award.

GOALS AND OUTCOMES

As you expand your project statement, consider the specific goals of your project. What is it that you hope to accomplish? What is the purpose or need for this research, and how will the funding support your work?

When you start to outline the goals of your research project, you may have strong, solid ideas, bullet points, or narratives that will be edited down into specific points. These points are a great way to start to align your goals with the project outcomes.

ASSESSMENT

The assessment or outcomes typically come at the end of research manuscripts in the discussion section after presenting the findings. Contrastingly, grant writing takes a backward approach. As you write out your goals, you need to align specific outcomes with each point. Consider these questions: *What deliverable will be accomplished with each goal? What activities will take place within each goal? How will you know if the grant was successful?* Can you answer them specifically both in writing and if someone asked you to explain your goals?

You need to think of the end at the beginning. This is because funders will look to see if you have considered how you will assess and evaluate your proposal by checking to see if the goals align with the outcomes. Describe how you plan to address your goals and use funds wisely. We elaborate on the assessment and evaluation more in later sections of the book.

Create a list of the three main things you hope to accomplish. Then, match an outcome for each goal. For example, if a goal is to analyze preexisting data by finding a relationship between museum attendance and age, what is a potential outcome of this analysis? You could state that a chart would be created to present how often people visit museums (frequency), and compare attendance rates by age. This could be further expounded to examine the differences between genders.

Continue this process by listing what types of additional data you could collect. Additionally, if you are using a public dataset you may be limited by what is available to you. Consider if there is some way to conduct a follow-up, interview participants, or compile a focus group to gather additional information to inform your project.

While many of these methods seem parallel to conducting scholarly research, the idea behind documenting your project is to show funders that you are cognizant about progress and revisions. Potential funders want to see that you are planning and preparing to manage your award. Even if your project is not successful, program officers and granting agencies appreciate knowing how you plan to meet your goals, and the steps you may take if your project is not successful.

Similar to conducting research, grant writing takes an immense amount of planning and preparation. The difference is that research can be organic, it can evolve, change, and shift as you conduct your investigation. When you write a grant proposal, you often cannot change what it is you propose to do. You are limited by the project statement and your stated goals. The funding is provided to support the ideas that you outline in your proposal.

If the grant project does not progress as you originally planned, you will have to let the funder know to keep them updated on any unanticipated changes. Many private foundations have shared that while they rarely pull their funds or stop supporting projects, there are extreme cases where this has happened. Program officers are especially cognizant of the challenges small organizations or individuals face with managing new grants and ask that any grantees be transparent with issues or concerns; for example, when a research project received funding but misappropriated funds, changed the focus of the project completely, or did not complete the promised deliverables. While these are examples of extreme cases, they are evidence for why it is so important to consider the end and the outcomes as you plan the beginning.

Some of the key terms included in your narrative should highlight the *history* of an existing music program, the *need* for a grant (to support a program or start a new one), the *purpose* of the new initiative, and the *outcomes* of the project that will be implemented. Using italics, bold font, or bullets will draw your readers' attention to key areas in your grant. This is especially important for smaller foundations that may receive several proposals and have to decide on a select few to share with the executive board.

INNOVATION AND COLLABORATION

In conversations that we have had with program officers and executive directors at various foundations and granting agencies, the one thing everyone is looking for is *innovation*. Funders want to know what makes your idea unique, different, and important. An innovative program or project does not have to be *new*—it can build off of something already in existence, borrow ideas or goals from another similar project, or be a reimagining of a project that is already in place.

In fact, many program officers have simply stated that they do not care if a program is identical to something else being done. They just want to know your story, your passion, and your idea. What makes your project worth funding? What makes it different? Program officers are generally very flexible and more concerned about the quality of the project than a perfectly written proposal. Remember that they are trying to find worthwhile projects to fund just as you are hoping to receive funding.

PERSONNEL

One of the areas that potential funders look for, which can also strengthen your grant application, is pursuing *meaningful collaborations*. These partnerships can be realized through collaborative projects with colleagues or larger grants that involve other universities, schools, organizations, or community centers. Even a scholarly grant such as the Fulbright Scholarship Award—which largely recognizes innovation in individual research—requires collaboration with the faculty at a university or college in an international setting.

As you prepare to apply for a grant, start to fine-tune your resume or curriculum vitae. Assess your own strengths and weaknesses. Consider the following questions: Do you have any publications that are related to the project you are trying to fund? Have you implemented a pilot program that you can discuss in the proposal? Are you actively involved in any collaborations within the community or amongst other organizations?

The personnel involved with a grant are integral to the success of your application. Reviewers will often consider the experience or knowledge base of those submitting an application. Some of the supplementary documents you will upload with your application include any relevant publications, an updated resume or CV, and additional files that demonstrate your expertise within the field. It is not unusual for a grant to be rejected because reviewers feel the PI is not experienced enough or well-versed in the field.

One way to address this dilemma is to build your collaborations within your discipline. Eliciting the support from university faculty or other professionals can augment your application by demonstrating your interest in partnering beyond your organization and your ability to work collaboratively. For example, if you are a classroom teacher applying for a grant for the first time, reach out to a neighboring community college or university to partner with a faculty member who will bring a different perspective to the grant application.

If you are a director at an organization or a scholar trying to receive funding for individual research, connect with individuals in the community who can provide resources to support your grant application. Many of these additional supplies and resources (e.g., the use of a designated space) can be included in the indirect costs. This will be further explained in the budget section of this book.

Including full professors, distinguished scholars, or experts in your discipline will bring added strength to your proposal. These individuals are typically well known in the field and may have already been awarded grants for their own research projects. When reviewers see someone who is more established, they are more likely to support your application. This is because there is a stronger guarantee that your grant will be successfully managed and implemented.

Senior faculty or distinguished scholars need only to be included on a grant for a small percentage. In this way, you are showing that you are building a team and collaborating. Including "experts" as consultants gives an added dimension to your grant application. Rarely do individuals receive an award when they are applying by themselves for the first time.

Writing grants as a team can be challenging unless you are comfortable working with fellow members and have good teamwork skills. Some people simply work better alone and can have difficulty collaborating with others. Team members bring different talents to the group and a team leader's ability to recognize these talents and bring out the best in people is a key to success. It is fine to recognize that some teams work better than others, but it is just as important to acknowledge that grant writing is inherently a collaborative field.

For example, every good guitar player knows that it is one thing to be able to play guitar well, but it is another to be able to play with others in a musical group. Musicians need to know when to turn down the sound, step up a riff, allow the drummer to fill in, or when to be silent. This ability to tune into the other players is what makes a great musical group—the synergy of musicians playing together.

This same collaborative process exists with the grant team. Each member of the grant team needs to know when to take the lead, when to turn down the communications, when to listen more, and when to allow others to communicate. Developing this ability to work in harmony is an essential component to building a successful and strong grant proposal.

Funders do not hesitate to indicate that they give preferences for collaborative projects. Many funders explicitly require collaboration with another institution that holds NFP status, while other funding agencies may state that a preference is given for collaborative research proposals.

Reaching out to individuals who are practicing or researching in your same areas (even if you have not personally met them) is a great way to build collaboration across states. It is an appealing prospect for a funder to think that a project they are supporting could have sustainability beyond just their community. This further increases your chances of not only receiving an award but pursuing additional funding after an initial grant is completed.

Throughout this book, we will continue to discuss the process of refining and shaping the project statement, and revising your own writing. In our experiences, we discovered that the more clearly you convey your ideas, tell your story, and present your project statement, the more likely you will be to receive a grant.

CHAPTER 3 NOTATIONS

1. There are six main components of any grant proposal even though the specific wording or language may differ amongst proposals.
2. Tell your story as you write and revise your project statement.
3. Match your goals with a potential funder's mission.
4. Think of the end at the beginning—consider your assessments as you write your goals.
5. Be collaborative and innovative with your project.

REFLECTION

Are you familiar with the thirty-second elevator speech concept? Imagine that you are in an elevator and the program officer for your potential funder enters the elevator. You have thirty seconds before the doors open to convince the program officer of the project statement, purpose, need, and focus of your grant. What would you say?

4

Recapitulation

Completing the Proposal

In its basic definition, a recapitulation is the act of summarizing the main points of an argument, making it an almost-perfect subheading for this chapter. In music, the recapitulation holds essentially the same definition—it is the part of a movement where the main themes from the opening (or exposition) are restated.

As we continue our discussion on developing and now, completing the proposal, it is important to remember that grant writing is perhaps the only time when repeating ideas is acceptable and expected. Being redundant in an effective manner is a key to writing a strong proposal. You are reiterating what you want to say, to remind your reader what it is you want to do.

Program officers at any funding agency may spend hours reading through your proposal, highlighting key points, and evaluating its potential for receiving funding. Remember that funders sometimes receive thousands of applications when an RFP is released. The more you restate, emphasize, and reiterate your points throughout, the more a potential funder will remember what it is you are planning to do with the grant.

Continue to draw the reader back to your main points. Reference statements that you make in your opening paragraph (perhaps connecting back to some of the descriptive statistics that you may have included in your project statement). Here are some strong phrases to use:

- Our project is innovative because. . .
- We propose a study that will. . .

- This project is of great importance to the field, because. . .
- We seek to identify. . .
- A lesser explored area is. . .
- Our proposed study directly relates to. . .
- This project will be conducted by a multidisciplinary team. . .

Using strong statements that continually reference your purpose, innovation, and collaboration will provide a strong thread throughout your proposal and continue to remind your reviewer of why your grant is important and worth funding.

GETTING TO THE DETAILS

Once you have written and revised your project statement to meet the specified requirements of the RFP, you will delve into building your proposal narrative, including (but not limited to) the following four components:

a. literature review
b. budget
c. timeline
d. evaluation and assessment

These sections will continue to support your project statement by shaping your narrative and telling a story. The literature review (a) provides supporting evidence for the need and value for this research and the budget (b) explains what funds you have, what funds you are requesting, and how you plan to allocate the funds.

The timeline (c) outlines who is involved, what you plan to do, where you plan to do it, when you plan to implement the project, why you need the funds, and how you will gather data and use funds appropriately, and the evaluation (d) describes how you will measure the success of your grant through evaluation and assessment.

In the following sections, each of these four components will be described in further detail with examples of key words, ideas, and suggestions for strengthening your proposal. Importantly, not every grant application will ask for these four components as stated here. Sometimes, the timeline will be included within a budget, or a literature review will be shortened into the introduction.

LITERATURE REVIEW

If any component of writing a grant proposal is going to align with scholarly research more than the project statement, it will be the literature review. This section is essentially the same process as building research to support the need and value for this project. As you write your project statement and develop your ideas, you probably have multiple scholarly sources to support your grant proposal.

However, grant writing does not always require the traditional scholarly articles. Consider that you can include statistical data, artifacts, evidence from the community, news highlights, or media interviews to support your proposal. For example, if you are submitting a grant for an after-school program, data on the challenges at-risk youth face on a daily basis could supplement research on the benefits of building and sustaining an after-school program.

The literature review should also not be tedious and heavy in description and research. Remember that the person reading your proposal may not necessarily have any background or expertise in the area in which you are seeking the grant. The program officers are hired to review proposals based on criteria that match the funder's RFP, not on the basis of being innovative researchers in your specialized field. The panel that reviews your grant will not necessarily be similar to an editorial committee at a journal.

Some larger government funders (such as NIH) may not even require a literature review. Instead, these RFAs or RFPs require a list of related publications from the PI and Co-PI to demonstrate expertise and experience in a given funding area. These may be in the form of an edited CV or a bio-sketch. In these instances, having established a strong track record of independent and collaborative research increases your chances of securing funding. Government agencies rarely fund individuals who do not have any documented expertise in an area in which they are seeking grants.

The greatest challenge then is finding a way to balance the scholarly research articles with more direct, accessible information that supports your ideas and need for funding. While many funders will provide you with an online application to fill out and submit as the grant proposal, others will simply state the components of the grant that need to be present and provide a limit on the narrative section. This can vary from being limited to 30,000 characters to ranging between twenty-five and fifty pages in length.

Consider these two examples:

(1) A private foundation based in Los Angeles, CA receives two hundred applications a year from small arts organizations and researchers. The proposals are each read and reviewed by a program officer who then

decides if the grant should be moved to the next stage of the review process and shared with funders. The application is a standardized, online application template that designates exact character and limited word count for each section.

(2) A new grant from the Department of Post-Secondary Education through the United States Department of Education (USDE) allows applicants a period of one month to submit an application. The RFP is vague in that anyone can submit a grant as long as the proposal meets the requirements specified by the USDE.

These include being an institution of higher education (IHE) and partnering with another IHE, using funds for a maximum of forty-eight months, demonstrating an ability to collect and analyze data effectively, and collaborate with the USDE to report findings in a timely fashion. The narrative section could be a maximum of thirty-five pages.

One of the main scholarly articles that faculty typically publish after graduating is condensing the dissertation into a twenty-page journal article. The process of editing and minimizing the literature review in that article is similar to writing a literature review (or providing supporting documentation) in a grant proposal. While brevity is important, you are essentially using this section to support everything you wrote in the project statement. The literature review is your harmony under your melody, grounding your ideas within a specific context.

BUDGET

Everyone's favorite part of writing and getting grants is the budget. Why? Because it's "all about the Benjamins," right? In fact, the budget is just as important to the proposal as your project statement. Many program officers have shared how they believe that the budget is often where they look first when reviewing applications. This is because it tells your story in a different way: identifying the individual components of the whole proposal.

The budget can also cause the most distress for anyone applying for a grant for the first time. Some questions could be as simple as these: "How much money can I ask for?" "What is allowed?" "How much is too much?" Trying to create a budget that is clear and concise shows the program officers or funding agencies that you have spent time planning and preparing for receiving this award.

One of our suggestions: don't be greedy. That is meant in the most direct and lighthearted way possible because while we *need* funds to support our research and projects, a funder *does* have those funds allocated to give. When planning your own budget, plan for less than the maximum dollar amount. We have found that a potential funder may be more willing (and eager) to fund your project when compared with someone who is asking for the exact amount allowed.

Granting agencies always report how many awards they have made each year and are very specific in the amount they will fund for each project. If you see an RFP for "up to $50,000" that means that the funds will never exceed $50,000. However, if you look through the granting history, you will most likely find that awarded grants ranged from $35,000 to $45,000, with a few being funded at the maximum amount.

Similarly, you should never budget for more than the allowed amount. This is showing a potential funder that you did not clearly outline how your grant money will be used and that you did not regard the guidelines provided in the RFP. Our suggestion is to always budget for around 85 percent of what is projected as an allowable amount.

Making Money Matter

The most important part of writing the budget is that you are making sure that all the funds you are asking for matter and are important to the grant. You do not want a reviewer, program officer, or panel questioning funds or hesitant that you will use funds appropriately. There are typically two components of the budget outline: the direct costs and the indirect costs. Unless you work at an institution or within an organization that already has a strong grants foundation, assistance for faculty, or a grants writer, much of this language is going to be unfamiliar to you.

The *direct costs* typically include the personnel fringe benefits—travel, equipment, supplies, transportation, and other direct costs that may be incurred. Think of it this way—the direct costs are everything that the grant money will be paying for directly, while the *indirect* costs are extra expenses that may be incurred during the implementation of the project. Figure 4.1 shows an example budget for a STEM (science, technology, engineering, and math) grant for classroom materials and professional development activities. The total allowable amount for the grant is $20,000. The total project income (direct costs) are $15,470.

The personnel are the principal investigator, any co-investigators, consultants who will be assisting with the project, data managers that could be responsible for collecting and managing all the data, administrative assistants who will help to manage the overall project, and graduate or undergraduate students who would be involved as additional support.

Fringe benefits are all those additional "perks" from your employer—holidays, sick leaves, or even the use of a company car. Any travel that may be completed during the duration of the grant (e.g., conference presentations) should also be calculated. Similarly, if you need special

PROJECT INCOME	STEM GRANT BUDGET				
DIRECT COST					
SALARIES					
	Title or Personnel	Number	Salary	%	Amount
	Science teacher	1	$ 62,000.00	7	$ 4,340.00
	Teaching assistant	1	$ 38,000.00	5	$ 1,900.00
TRAVEL					
	Conference registration $150	2			$ 300.00
	Airfare $200/each ticket	2 roundtrip			$ 400.00
	Hotel room $125/each room	2 rooms 1/night			$ 250.00
MATERIALS					
	Smart Boards $1,265 per room	2			$ 2,530.00
	iPads for students $500 each	6			$ 3,000.00
	STEM workshop	2			$ 600.00
	Multimedia	1			$ 150.00
	Laptop	1			$ 800.00
CONSULTANTS					
	STEM consultant	2	$150/hour	8 hrs	$ 1,200.00
	University faculty				
TOTAL COSTS					**$ 15,470.00**

Figure 4.1. Budget Example

equipment (such as video cameras or digital recorders), office supplies, or postage, make sure to calculate the exact costs.

Some large government grants (such as NIH) may even allow for the purchase of a computer to store all the data that will be collected. In fact, much of the funding available in the sciences allows for the purchase of large electronic equipment to store sensitive data. However, the requests have to match the research project. A potential funder will become suspicious if you ask for $6,000 to purchase ten flip cameras to collect data in an elementary school.

Try to search for the exact items online and calculate exact numbers when planning your budget. If you know there is a conference you want to attend next year, search for potential flights online and include the cost of taxis, meals, and hotels. Be as specific as possible. This shows funders you have taken the time to research and plan how the funds will be used. The funding agencies will appreciate that you are being conscientious about using the funds appropriately.

Additionally, some agencies may require matching funds from the organization or individual applying for a grant. These funds can come from various sources including cash, salary time, donations, or funds from other institutions supporting your project. Typically, the match is structured as a 1:1 ratio. If you are requesting $1,000 for a project, you need to demonstrate that you have $1,000 already allocated for this project.

If you are a faculty member, the match can come from a course load reduction or a faculty development grant. If you are the director at an organization, the match can come from another grant source, donations, or your own time on salary above what you are asking to be covered through the grant. Additionally, some funders will require that the matching funds cannot be used from other awards. For example, the National Endowment for the Arts, which is well known for requiring a match for their grants, specifies that the matched funds cannot come from another government grant or agency.

Even if a funder does not require a match, demonstrating additional support for your project will strengthen your proposal. For example, if you are seeking to expand an instrumental music program for upper elementary students, include any existing funds from the school, fund-raising efforts from students, and any use of space, faculty, or resources from community centers or local colleges. Matching funds are important because they demonstrate sustainability of a project even after awarded funds are complete.

There are also specific requirements for what is allowed under indirect costs. Many grant proposals will not even allow for indirect costs while others require a percentage to be included in the budget. This section may also be called the match, overhead, or in-kind contributions.

Indirect costs are associated with the funds needed to keep a program or project functioning. Some examples include utilities, use of a building or space, advertising, donations, accounting, and insurance. Many times, a percentage of the indirect costs are already negotiated by the school or university and is applied as overhead for administration or maintenance fees.

Including administrators during the grant writing process is important in aligning the budgetary needs for your project with the documented budget for a university. Even if you are not required to list your indirect costs, you should create a list for your own records so that you can continue to maintain how any funds are being used when the project is awarded.

The budget is dependent on what the funder allows. Some granting agencies will provide a template for you to fill out, asking you to calculate the direct and indirect costs involved with the project. Other times, the funder will simply ask that a budget narrative is included within the proposal.

Sometimes you are asked to submit both a narrative and an itemized list. The narrative is simply a detailed description of the funds being requested, with information on why the funds are important for each component of the budget. For example, if you are the principal investigator on a grant and you are asking for 5 percent of salary time from the budget, you may have to explain all of the different responsibilities that you will assume throughout the project, thereby justifying the amount being requested.

Additionally, an itemized list is simply that—a list of each item in the budget and the correlating amount. In this instance, if you are going to be asking for 5 percent salary time, the 5 percent would need to be calculated from your gross salary and included in the itemized list. The itemized list should also include a justification. This is a short description explaining what the funds will be used for. Make sure to always include this with your budget. The justification is essentially as it appears—you are justifying your budget request.

As an example, let us assume your salary is $54,000. You would be requesting 5 percent of salary time to work on this grant. How will your 5 percent effort be implemented during the award? Some examples include stating that you will spend one day a week managing the grant, contacting personnel at sites, or preparing reports.

If you decide that your level of effort will be 5 percent of your time, this means that you need to request $2,700 as part of your specific line item. Some people think that allocating time or effort in a grant means that the money is then deducted from your salary. In fact, this means that you are essentially receiving external funding to support your time and effort on this project. Your university or institution is not spending money on you.

Be cautious of how much time you may be allowed to commit to additional projects or any research supported with external funding. For example, you may only be allowed one course reduction from your teaching load or a specific amount of funds from your employer. If that is the case, then indicate how much money you are requesting (e.g., $2,700) and indicate that the funds are to be used to support a one-course teaching reduction from your faculty load.

Think of it this way: you are a full-time faculty member at a large university. The university draws on endowments and external funding to pay your salary. However, if you bring in funds from your own grant, you are essentially saving the university from having to support you. This is why many faculty and scholarly positions require external funding. The university does not want to have to find places to pay for your salary. And, if you are 100 percent funded from grants, imagine that you could essentially be a faculty member at any institution of your choice.

How much you request is also contingent on how many funds are available, how much time you will dedicate on this project, and the number of other individuals involved. If you are applying for a $100,000 grant and there are five people who will be involved, you cannot request 25 percent salary time for each individual. This will quickly use up the available funds and create an imbalance in your budget request of direct costs. Categorizing everyone's time and involvement will help you plan a budget, allocate funds, and create a timeline.

As you plan the budget and list the personnel involved, outline individual responsibilities and the approximate time it would take to manage and implement the designated tasks. Typically, the PI and Co-PI are placed for 15–20 percent of their time, while additional researchers and managers are listed around 5–10 percent, with assistants or senior faculty who provide consultations ranging from 2–5 percent of their time.

Some government grants will specify that any senior faculty or consultants cannot request funds greater than 50 percent of their own salary. This is to ensure that any awards are not applied directly toward salaries and are instead allocated toward materials, supplies, or other project costs. Typically, senior faculty or distinguished scholars are only included for a small percentage on grants, to provide their expertise rather than secure additional funding.

Remember that a budget can change. Sometimes program officers will reach out to you after you submit the proposal to suggest modifications to a budget, or your own personnel or position may change prior to receiving an award. The important thing here is to be transparent with any changes in requested funds when communicating with the funder. This ensures that there are no confusions or assumptions during the grant management process.

TIMELINE

Many people tend to overlook the relevance of writing and completing a timeline because there is always a greater focused placed on the project statement or the budget. However, the timeline tells the funder two things. First, it shows that you have planned every step of how you will use the funds. Second, it shows the funder what deliverables they can expect and when to expect them.

Your timeline should explain *who, what, where,* and *when*. The *who* describes who will be implementing the research project, collecting data, analyzing, and writing final reports. The *what* describes the actions or activities that will be done each week, month, and year. The *where* explains the setting and context for the project, and the *when* shows the funder the days, weeks, or months that create a structure and foundation for the grant. The timeline demonstrates how you will *implement* the grant by presenting key areas of outcomes.

When considering *who* is involved in the grant, you should make sure to address two important points. The first is who is involved directly with the implementation of the project, that is, the PI, Co-PI, and any consultants or data managers. Second, the *who* also includes the individual receiving the funds or the community that is directly benefiting from any services. For example, if the grant is to support and extend community relations through an outreach effort at a hospital, the *who* is not only the investigators but also the families participating in the project.

Grant writing is a redundant process. You may often feel like you are saying the same things over and over again; however, that is expected both to reiterate what it is you are trying to accomplish and how you plan to achieve your goals. The *what* includes the specific different parts of the grant that you intend to accomplish. Ask yourself, *what am I going to do*? You need to show funders exactly what it is that you intend to do with the funds that they have awarded. This includes any initial contact with participants, data collection, initial reports, visitations, observations, or analysis.

Remember that the timeline is also showing funders exactly *where* the money is going—that is, where the project will take place. This describes if the project will be at a school, in a community setting, observing student participation, implementing professional development, or analyzing preexisting data sets.

Finally, your timeline should be specific in showing different time points throughout the process. The *when* are the periods during which there will be outcomes delivered. The outcomes can be formative or summative, but should represent how you continue to pursue the originally stated goals. If your time points are too large, potential funders will wonder why it may take so long to accomplish any tasks. If the time points are too close together, potential funders may question if you are able to look at the big picture.

Let us analyze an example to better understand this process. Table 4.1 shows the first year of a timeline that has been written to explain the *who, what, where,* and *when* for a project that will collect data through a hospital's community outreach program. The project is seeking funding for two years to establish partnerships with families within the neighboring community. The hospital personnel will assist single mothers in caring for their newborns. However, there are three major points that need to be fixed in this example to strengthen the timeline.

First, the timeline has very long periods between deliverables. Rather than focusing on six-month intervals, this two-year long project could demonstrate what goals will be met at every three months. Then examples of smaller goals every month can be inserted into each section. The timeline can then be broken up into four equal sections for each year.

Table 4.1. Timeline for Project Implementation

Date	*Activity*	*Outcome*
June 1, 2015 – November, 2015	Grant funds released to university Planning meetings with group Contact sites for data collection and study participants	Allocate funds at the research center and distribute funds to consultants Finalize data collection
December 15, 2015	Planning meeting for responsibilities and activities	Distribute interview and survey information to on-site managers Categorize data
January 15, 2016 – May 2016	Preliminary investigation of hypothesis and research question 1	Analysis of research question 1 to be completed by May 2016
June 1, 2016	Planning meetings to discuss findings from first year	Distribute funds for second year of grant/contact granting agency to confirm allocation of remaining funds for year two

For example, the first few months could be focused on securing sites, contacting potential participants, and training personnel to work with families. At the end of each month within this first quarter of the year, listing key deliverables will add detail and depth to the larger grant proposal. Funders will understand what to expect at the end of the three months and see how you will be achieving those goals.

Second, there are no specific examples of the types of data that will be collected. While it is important to list that you will collect and analyze data, you should include what data will be collected, from which sources, and how and when the data will be analyzed. Additionally, your deliverable or outcome for that time period could be a formative report, the results of a meeting with all of the stakeholders in the group, or submitting presentations to conferences or seminars.

Finally, the timeline should list specific dates. While it is important to show that you are planning for the trajectory of the grant, you should not generalize dates and deliverables. For example, if you plan to recruit participants and provide training for personnel within the first three months, be specific about when these different activities will take place. Do not simply state that everything will be done within an ambiguous period of time. This leaves funders confused and concerned.

Table 4.2. Revised Timeline

Date	*Activity*	*Outcome*
June 1, 2015	Grant funds released to university	Allocate funds at the research center and distribute funds to consultants
August 1, 2015	Organize planning meeting to discuss goals and outline of grant implementation	Outline data collection procedures
September 1, 2015	Contact sites for data collection and invite program/research participants	Finalize data collection sites and program participants
November 15, 2015	Plan for conference presentations for the first year	Submit abstracts for conference presentation/proceedings
December 15, 2015	Planning meeting for responsibilities and activities	Distribute interview and survey information to on-site managers and categorize data collection for time point #1 (interviews, surveys, case study participants)
January 15, 2016	Preliminary investigation of hypothesis and research question 1	Analysis of research question 1 to be completed by May 2016
March 30, 2016	Analyze and code qualitative data and conduct t-tests and chi-square tests and gather and organize demographic data	Preliminary report to granting agency
June 1, 2016	Planning meetings to discuss findings from first year of analysis and results from research question 1	Distribute funds for second year of grant/contact granting agency to confirm allocation of remaining funds for year two. Follow-up with participants for subsequent data collection (time points #2 and #3)

In Table 4.2, let us compare a revised version of the initial timeline. Here we see more details and descriptions that align with each time period of the grant for the first year. Not only is the revised version more specific and clear, but it provides examples of dates (months and year), activities (to achieve goals), and deliverables (to present outcomes).

Even if an RFP does not specifically ask for a timeline or table, organizing your process into a table such as the one presented here will demonstrate your ability to plan, implement, and manage any potential funds. Remember that the timeline is simply a summary of your grant proposal. Your narratives explain why the project is important, while the timeline shows how the information is organized.

Recall our opening definition of a recapitulation—the process of summarizing the main points. Your timeline is the recapitulation of your grant proposal, outlining what it is you will do, every step of the way. This will help ensure to the reader that you have a well-organized and planned approach.

EVALUATION AND ASSESSMENT

The final section of the grant application is the evaluation. If the timeline demonstrates how you will *implement* the grant, the evaluation demonstrates how you will *measure* the success of the grant by gathering data throughout the process. Although the evaluation is often written at the end of the grant proposal, it is important to think about the evaluation as being ongoing, connecting to your goals, and demonstrated through your outcomes. In this sense, you are thinking about the end of the proposal at the beginning.

This can often be described as a backward process of writing and planning. The evaluation ultimately determines if you were successful in achieving your goals, demonstrates the viability of a program, and outlines any specific areas of weakness for future implementation. The process can ensure that you stay on course and meet your deadline.

In Figure 4.2 we present an example of a backward timeline using a PERT chart. PERT stands for program evaluation review technique. These charts are often utilized for large projects and assist with the planning, scheduling, and implementation of a project. A PERT chart is particularly useful if you have large numbers of individuals involved with a grant project.

Thinking about the end at the beginning shows you are thoughtful about your grant—that you are planning, preparing, and managing the funds that you will be awarded. Too often the evaluation or assessment component is an afterthought, and that always shows in the way that this section is written. However, describing how the outcomes are measured with both formative and summative data is just as important (Rajan, 2014).

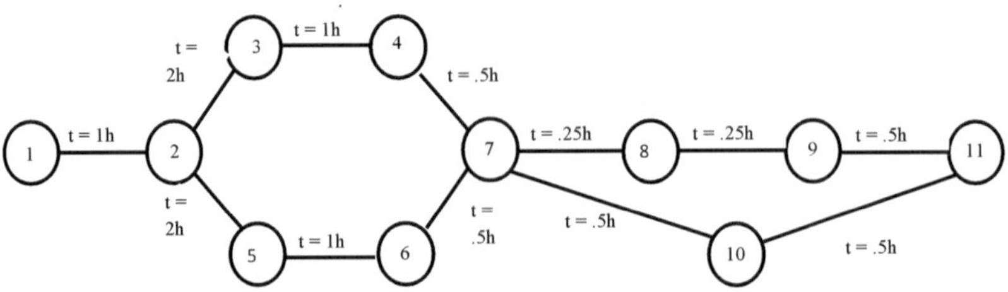

1. Prepare statistical design
2. Prepare final copy of instrument
3. Collect data
4. Assemble all statistical data
5. Continue updating literature review
6. Finish final update of literature review
7. Begin write-up of data analysis
8. Run descriptive statistics on data
9. Begin write-up of data analysis
10. Write up final results
11. Review final results with chairperson

Figure 4.2. Example of a Backward Timeline Using a PERT Chart

You will also need to consider what types of data you may be collecting to support your evaluation. Primary data collection could include both qualitative and quantitative data; however, a secondary analysis of an existing data set only allows for quantitative reporting (Rajan, 2014).

In your budget narrative or justification, you should indicate who is responsible for the data collection and analysis for the evaluation section of the grant. This should be clearly distinguished from any data you may be collecting as part of the research project that you are seeking to fund. The evaluation could be either internal or external. If the evaluation will be conducted internally, this usually means you are responsible for the data collection and analysis for the evaluation, or one of the Co-PIs is assuming this role within the grant.

If the evaluation is to be conducted externally, you will need to ensure that you allow for funding for the evaluator. The evaluator may be an independent consultant, an assessment expert, or another colleague or scholar who you want involved in the project for his or her expertise. Smaller grants usually do not require a huge evaluation section but these funders still want to ensure that you are systematically documenting the progress of your award.

Typically, an external evaluator is allowed 5–10 percent of the total grant awarded. This needs to be included in detail within the budget section of your grant as well. If the timeline explains the *who, what, where,* and *when* of the grant, and your project statement is the *why,* the evaluation is the *how.*

While an internal evaluation can be considerably cheaper, the persons responsible for conducting the evaluation within the grant should be able to demonstrate experience in data collection, measurement, and assessment. Additionally, the evaluation should match the research questions. If the project is primarily qualitative in nature, having an evaluation focused on statistical measures may seem confusing to potential funders. Furthermore, there is no need to include tables and figures in your evaluation section unless they are completely necessary. Remember, that your entire proposal should continue to tell a story—from the beginning to the end.

An external evaluator may have specific requirements of what is needed to conduct the evaluation. Find individuals who are willing to commit to this role if your grant is funded. Do not assume that someone will be willing to take on the role of an evaluator just because you have been awarded a grant. The evaluation is a detailed process that has to align with the goals and outcomes of the project itself.

If you plan to invite an external evaluator as an independent consultant, you need to have an itemized budget plan from the evaluator to include within your own larger budget. Some evaluators will include travel, office supplies, and other daily expenses as part of their budget. An evaluator may also be subcontracted through your organization or institution. Many government grants will require an external evaluator or even conduct their own evaluation of your project. Regardless of whether the evaluation is internal or external, an explanation of how the evaluation connects to the larger grant is needed in the proposal.

Many grant proposals do not give guidelines for the evaluation section. Some funders only require an explanation of how program evaluation will be conducted to demonstrate ongoing evaluation and assessment both during and after the project concludes. This is often frustrating for scholars and researchers who are unsure of the process in which to conduct the evaluation. Sometimes, we are left wondering what it is the funder is looking for within the evaluation section or how we can "prove" we have been successful.

Your evaluation section should demonstrate how you will be assessing the strength of the project both during and after its completion. Think of the evaluation as a mini research project. Create a bulleted list of your original goals and ideas for how you will assess your success. What types of additional data can you gather, and how will that data inform your findings? Before starting your evaluation section, consider the following four questions:

1. What are the main goals of this project?
2. What are the main outcomes of this project?
3. Who is involved with implementing/managing this project?
4. Who/what will be the focus of this project?

Sometimes, you will already know what your outcomes will be while other times, you have proposed ideas for what you want to accomplish with grant funding. Question 1 shapes your entire proposal and question 2 determines if you were successful in meeting your goals.

Question 3 will be the people helping to construct and implement the evaluation (and sometimes that is also the principal investigator), while question 4 shows where, and from what sources, you can collect supporting evidence. These can be different documents, communities, or individuals who are the recipients of a program or project.

Let us consider the following example. You are implementing a research project that explores student involvement and engagement with attending a live musical performance. The performance is being presented by a local community orchestra. The students attending the performance are all in third grade. There are two classrooms and two teachers. There are a total of fifty-six students participating in this project.

The main goals of the project are (1) to explore student perceptions as audience members at a live performance, and (2) student interest in participating in musical activities. *How might you begin to shape the evaluation section?* If you are already collecting data from students (journals and interviews), *what additional data would be needed in an evaluation section?* Here, you might include focus group discussions with those involved with the grant implementation, or interviews and surveys of teacher perceptions. In this example, some of the evaluation data might also come from the students.

Consider another example, a research project to create a new website as a professional development resource for university faculty who are advising doctoral students. Funding might be used for consultants, web designers, and data managers. Funding could also be allotted to faculty time given to developing specific areas of the website for content expertise. *What would be some components of the evaluation?*

The university faculty could be engaged in a pre-assessment of their needs for a professional development resource, and then a post-assessment of their ability to navigate the completed product. Faculty could also be asked to critique the newly designed website and provide feedback for what could be changed, strengthened, or added to make the website more comprehensive. A survey that is distributed at three different time points could also serve as a component of the evaluation section.

Remember that evaluation is not about whether something was done right; it is about examining what was done, and what could be done better. The findings of your evaluation can always be used in an additional grant application. You could potentially demonstrate that the goal of the original grant was met but that additional funding is needed to strengthen the project based on findings from faculty feedback and the evaluation of the project.

Ultimately, funders are not as concerned about your meeting all the goals, rather they want to see that you are thinking about how you may achieve your goals, what you are doing to meet your outcomes, and the ways in which you are willing to document your process. Evaluating your own work also shows potential funders that you are willing to grow, take revisions, and make changes to fit the funder's needs (and not just your own). This process will then inform future funding, suggest revisions, and help measure the sustainability of a program or project.

Completing the literature review, budget, timeline, and evaluation will take you one step closer to finishing your grant application. As you review each section, make sure to reference your introduction, ensuring connections between your originally stated goals and the outcomes you describe in the timeline and evaluation.

Remember that the language used in some grant applications may not directly reflect the inclusion of a literature review or an evaluation section. However, funders will look to see that you have planned on how to assess your grant, that you have determined how funds will be used, and that you can demonstrate the activities and outcomes that will take place at the various stages of your proposal.

In the next chapter, we discuss some strategies and techniques for editing, revising, and writing your proposal. Anyone who writes for a profession will tell you that revisions are often the hardest part of completing a project. These ideas are tools that are both common in the grant writing field and strategies that we have employed.

CHAPTER 4 NOTATIONS

1. The literature review is not just a review of literature—this section can include various types of supporting documents and evidence to strengthen your proposal.
2. Do not be greedy in your budget section—try to allow for around 85 percent of the allowable amount.
3. Think of the timeline as your *who, what, where, when,* and *how.*
4. The evaluation can be internal, external, or both. Include formative and summative assessments.
5. Do not hesitate to repeat your ideas throughout your proposal. Grant writing allows for being redundant and restating points.

REFLECTION

Imagine that a private funder approached you with the idea to support a research project. You are allowed $30,000 for each year for three years (a total of $90,000). What are the main components of the budget that you will list for your first draft? What will be in your direct and indirect costs? Additionally, how might you organize the ways which you would use these funds in a timeline? Apply these questions to an actual research project that you are developing.

5

Finale

Revising and Editing the Proposal

The ability to write succinctly and clearly is one of the skills to becoming a successful grant writer. Writing a grant proposal is similar to writing other types of papers and manuscripts, and with that process comes the need for the cycle of revising, editing, and revising. In musical compositions, musicians are often told, "Don't bore us, get to the chorus." In grant writing, you need to get to the point—fast.

One of the best ways to enhance your skills in effective writing is to begin with an understanding of some of the most common mistakes we make when writing grant proposals. Figure 5.1 illustrates the top ten reasons for ineffective writing. For example, make sure that active voice versus passive voice is used. Active voice is "Susan viewed the information" versus "The information was reviewed by Susan." Active voice is generally more brisk, concise, and structured.

It is difficult to write in any subject matter and avoid the temptation to use jargon. A major reason that grant proposal reviewers assign a low evaluation rating for a proposal is simply because they do not understand content that is being written and the use of jargon is often the major culprit.

Editing is another important component of the writing process. By the time the comprehensive grant proposal is written, you may be tired and just want to meet the deadline in submitting the application. However, this is not the time to shortchange yourself and avoid proper editing. When editing the grant proposal you should be concerned with subject-verb agreement, proper use of pronouns, grammar, sentence structure, tone, and ensuring that the writing is concise and error-free.

Writing Term		Description of Term
1. Academic background	→	Failure to develop writing skills in school
2. Communication style differences	→	Using the wrong communication style or overly using one style
3. Hedging and jargon	→	Using unclear abbreviations, acronyms, or jargon
4. Lack of planning	→	Failure to develop a cue outline
5. Lack of editing	→	Premature submission of the grant proposal without proper editing
6. Using wrong tone	→	Selecting words that create a negative impression
7. Using ascending versus descending approach	→	Using inductive writing style versus a deductive writing style
8. Creating an clear budget	→	Writing a confusing or inaccurate budget plan
9. Focusing on the problem versus the solution	→	Overly emphasizing the problem versus proposed solutions in the proposal
10. Using passive versus active writing	→	Using passive instead of active voice

Figure 5.1. Ten Reasons for Ineffective Writing

The use of abbreviations, colons, dashes, pronouns, spacing, grammar, verbs, adjectives, prepositions, and interjections all play an important role in effective writing. In other words, grant writing is like Revising Writing 101. Many scholars are encouraged to use long statements, ambiguous terms, or "fancy" language to express their viewpoints. In grant writing, the ability to write short sentences and paragraphs, omit needless words, and select simple and meaningful words to illustrate your points is much more desirable.

Your writing style might also be attributed to your communication style. For example, one of the most popular theories of communication style was formulated by Carl Jung, a renowned psychoanalyst. As an outgrowth of Jung's work, he identified four primary communication styles: *Intuitor, Feeler, Thinker,* and *Doer.*

While each of us have and use these four communication styles, we tend to have a dominant style in our writing. The *Intuitor* writing style places emphasis on creativity and originality, but tends to be wordier, and present content in an unrealistic and dogmatic manner. The *Feeler* communication style is personal and expressive, but may be written in an overdramatic and emotional manner.

The *Thinker* communication style is one that presents information in an organized and structured manner but may tend to be verbose, rigid, too structured, and over detailed. The last communication style, the *Doer,* tends to be spirited and down to earth, short and concise, but may tend to be too short, direct, and lack thoroughness and creativity. You must recognize your dominant style in grant writing and ensure that you do not overemphasize your style, which leads to ineffective writing.

For example, if you are a *Thinker,* be careful that your writing is not too in-depth, detailed, or overly structured, which may work against you in presenting your ideas to the grant reviewers. Likewise, if you have the dominant communication style of the *Intuitor,* you may come across as being too unstructured, scattered in your thoughts, illogical, and hard to understand.

When writing with the dominant style of the *Feeler,* make sure that you do not over dramatize and personalize your writing. This may distract the grant proposal reviewers from the content. Lastly, if your dominant style is the *Doer,* be cautious that your writing is not too assertive. You may come across to the grant reviewers as being too shortsighted and lacking in creativity.

CHOOSING YOUR WORDS

Sometimes, we are so accustomed to using abbreviations, we confuse terms in our scholarly works. For instance, the use of "e.g." is commonly used before an actual example, whereas "i.e." is typically used to mean "in place of" or "in other words." Understanding how these terms are used can help make the difference between a quality document and one that is distracting to the reader. (Some other common mistakes in grant writing are illustrated in Figure 5.2.)

You might also want to select words that are more positive than negative. The use of "unhappy" versus "not happy," "prefer" versus "does not like," "self-reliant" versus "defiant," and "opportunity" versus "a problem," can be subtle differences in the word selection, but produce a more receptive atmosphere for the grant reviewer.

Adapt versus Adopt	The word "adapt" means "to adjust yourself to" and "adopt" is "to choose as your own."
et al. versus etc.	"et al." refers to "and others" and "etc." means "and so forth."
Eminent versus Imminent	"Eminent" means "outstanding" and "imminent" means "about to happen."
Percent versus Percentage	"Percent" is "per hundred" and "percentage" is "a proportion of a whole," such as a percentage of total.
Among versus Between	The word "between" is used to describe a comparison between two items whereas "among" describes comparisons of three or more items.
e.g. versus i.e.	"e.g.," is used for an example whereas "i.e.," is used in place of "in other words."
Further versus Farther	"Further" is a larger extent and "farther" means distance.
Accept versus Except	"Accept" means to receive or agree with whereas "except" means to exclude something.

Figure 5.2. Common Mistakes in Grant Proposal Writing

You should always ensure that your writing includes simple and direct words. For example, "begin" versus "commence," "end" versus "terminate," "consider" versus "give consideration to," "please" versus "we would like to request that," "use" versus "utilize," "agree" versus "concur," or "try" versus "endeavor to."

Try not to focus too much on the problem versus the solutions. While it is important that you illustrate that you have a sound understanding of the problem, the focus needs to be on the solution. Present the problem, and if possible the root cause of the problem, and then focus primarily on your solution or approach in solving the issue.

ORGANIZING THE PROPOSAL

The best way to plan the grant proposal is to follow the actual outline of the grant application. Typically most grant proposals are constructed in a logical manner starting with a summary, introduction, problem statement, objectives, project method, evaluation, and cost description. Even if you do not agree with the way an application is organized, do not reformat or change the application. Each granting agency spends a lot of time determining what format works for them and for each RFP they release.

When preparing the proposal, plan your content in an organized manner using a "cue" outline. A cue outline is used when you write your major points in an outline, which then later can be developed into the grant proposal. Starting with the major headings and subheadings can give you the necessary structure that you need in planning the proposal.

When developing a *cue outline* you must organize the material that is most suitable for the grant proposal. Figure 5.3 illustrates common strategies in organizing a grant proposal. For example, if you are explaining the historical background of your institution, you will probably use this strategy and start by the date in which the institution was formed until the present.

The *topical technique* can be an effective strategy. This technique consists of arranging your topics in a manner that is sequential. For example, if you are describing the parts of a presentation, you would most likely use a topical approach whereby you start with the opening, followed by the delivery, and then the closing.

Consider also the *general-to-specific* organization strategy. This strategy would be sensible to use when describing a large field of study then narrowing down to a detailed item. For example, if you are describing the many types of disciplinary techniques used in an organizational setting, you then would narrow down to the specific type of disciplinary technique that is the focus of the project by using the general-to-specific approach. Another example: describing an entire organization in a general fashion and then narrowing the topic to specifically focus on one department.

The use of the *strategy of complexity* is used when you are writing about a highly detailed subject. In this situation you would begin by describing the least complex items and then proceeding to the most complex items. In

Strategies	Description of Strategy
Chronological	Information ordered by date or time.
Topical	Arranging information one topic to another.
General to specific	Presenting broad information then to narrow terms.
Complexity	Arranging the most-to-least complex content.
Familiarity	Arranging information in order from most to least familiar.
Utility	Presenting information in order from the most useful to least useful.
Acceptability	Presenting information in order of most acceptable to least acceptable.
Hierarchal	Structuring content according to rank or level.

Figure 5.3. Strategies for Organizing a Grant Proposal

this manner the reader is more likely to understand the information you are presenting and follow it in a logical manner that is understandable.

Like complexity, *familiarity* is a strategy where you would write about the least familiar items and then narrow down to the most familiar items. The *utility strategy* is a similar approach; you begin to write about the least useful items and then narrow down to the most useful items from a utility standpoint.

The *acceptability strategy* is also a common approach used in organizing a grant proposal. This strategy begins by presenting information that is anticipated to be most acceptable to the reader and then focusing on the least acceptable. An example is asking for funding to imitate a project and then instead of showing internal funding sustainability, requesting additional funding from the grant source.

THE PERSUASIVE PROPOSAL

Much of how we write grant proposals is to inform and persuade the reader to support our ideas and give us funding. It is important to provide information to the reader and to also prompt the reader to act in a positive way to your request. When persuading a reader to act upon something, there are several strategies that you should keep in mind.

Write in a pleasant but natural manner, being creative, appealing to their senses, avoiding objections, and writing with positive statements. It is also critical that you use proper grammar and composition so that you produce a quality document and one that is not distracting to the reader. We cannot stress the importance of having strong grammar, punctuation, and writing composition skills. Remember, the funders are reading this proposal—how you write will impact their decision on whether to award funding. Figure 5.4 provides some characteristics of effective writing, including tone, composition, voice, and rhythm.

Tone can be described as the feelings or atmosphere you create by the actual words you select. Generally you want to select words that create an even-tempered feeling versus an overly dramatic or formal atmosphere.

The *composition* refers to composing the information so that it is purposeful and comprehensive. Composition includes concern for the audience, the type of outline, formulation of ideas and information, and the format presented. In preparing your composition, ask questions such as these:

- Who is my audience?
- What do they need to know?
- How familiar are they with the language and subject?
- How should the information be presented?
- How can I keep the reader engaged?

Effective *movement* entails the length of sentences and paragraphs. Make sure that sentences are concise and that paragraphs are generally only three to five sentences long. It is better to err on brevity than being too verbose. Sentences should move from point to point in a smooth and natural manner.

The use of proper voice and rhythm can help ensure the writing is clear, succinct, and understandable. Consider again our musical analogies. Rhythm helps drive a song or a piece of music. Similarly, the use of voice in writing should be natural and genuine, without the use of pretentious words and phrases. Sentences should be consistent and clear. These will all ensure that your narrative flows well and contains good rhythm.

Structure	• Follow grant proposal guidelines • Present in an organized manner • Be concise but clear
Tone	• Ensure natural writing • Use even-tempered words • Avoid drama or generalizations
Composition	• Use active writing versus passive writing • Avoid repetition • Include references and sources to support content
Movement	• Use short sentences and paragraphs • Be concise and succinct • Move smoothly from point-to-point
Format	• Edit any jargon • Ensure tables conform to required style manual • Use simple and visually attractive format
Voice	• Use natural based conversational style • Use genuine sounding style that is not pretentious • Avoid stilted style
Rhythm	• Sentences should be clear and flow well • Edit glaring errors and jargon • Be consistent in writing
Grammar	• Ensure proper mechanics and punctuation • Keep writing free of errors • Follow required manual style
Illustrations	• Use clear, neat, legible tables and charts • Be consistent in format and descriptions • Keep numbers aligned properly

Figure 5.4. Characteristics of Effective Writing (Adapted with permission from Grant and Tomal 2013)

Proper *formatting* includes the fundamental design of the proposal, line spacing, headings and subheadings, and visuals. A rule of thumb is to use a simple but attractive format. The format makes a major impression on the reader; if the format is weak, the reader may think the content is weak as well. The last characteristics of effective writing include grammar and illustrations. Make sure that you use proper mechanics and punctuation and that the writing is free from errors.

Remember that your ability to write in a concise manner, to edit, and proofread your material requires patience and concentration. Hyphens are often misused or omitted by grant writers. A hyphen should be used when there are compound adjectives. Some examples of this include "year-long study," "state-of-the-art equipment," "first-rate session," "long-range objective," and "year-end results."

Make sure to double-check all basic principles of punctuation are being used and that the quality of writing meets the standards of the grant institution. Some principles of effective writing follow:

- Use concise and simple language.
- Use short sentences and paragraphs.
- Delete unneeded words.
- Use active voice versus passive voice.
- Eliminate any needless repetition.
- Eliminate any jargon.
- Use effective tone for your reader.
- Include effective transitions from one thought to another.
- Provide information in an orderly and acceptable manner for the reader.
- Include charts and tables to illustrate your material.
- Use asterisks, bullets, and numbers to emphasize information.
- Be consistent in using terms, phrases, titles, and subtitles.

Make sure to set your margin and line spacing in accordance with the grant proposal requirements. Many grant proposals prefer that one- to one-and-a-half-inch margins are used. This allows the reader to make notes in the margins. Often the right margin is unjustified, which will allow the sentences to appear more natural. Justifying the right margin often causes odd spacing between the words and may distract the reader.

Although this may seem an obvious suggestion, make sure you use the formatting capabilities on your computer. Use strong subheadings, which serve as an effective roadmap for the reader. Headings and subheadings are needed to guide the reader through your proposal. In some applications, the headings are already provided.

If you choose to include any tables, figures, or charts, make sure you *need* them. The purpose of a table is to succinctly present large amounts of information in a simplified and easily readable manner. This allows the reader to rapidly compare numerical text and data without reading several paragraphs. Do not simply include tables that list demographics or statistics that are not relevant or vital to your proposal.

BACK TO THE BASICS

Sometimes, no matter how many papers we have written, it is important to get back to the basics of writing, sentence structure, and grammar. There are many ways to construct sentences and paragraphs. The writer has a choice selecting and integrating the many parts of the English language: *nouns, verbs, pronouns, adverbs, adjectives, prepositions, conjunctions,* and so on. Having a sound understanding and being skillful in the use of the English language can make the difference between an outstanding proposal and a mediocre one. Remember some basic guidelines of writing.

- Subjects are always nouns or pronouns.
- Nouns are places, people, things, concepts, and so on.
- Verbs express the action part of a sentence.
- Pronouns take the place of a noun.
- Adjectives modify or qualify a noun or pronoun.
- Adverbs describe verbs.

The *structure* of a sentence can either be simple or compound. Simple sentences are generally short and concise but give sufficient detailed information. Compound sentences generally consist of more than two independent clauses without subordinate clauses. While compound sentences are acceptable, the use of simple sentences generally is more effective in writing grant proposals.

The principles of effective writing can be summarized by following the five Cs. These consist of *concise, completeness, courtesy, clarity,* and *correctness.* Keeping these five Cs in mind can help you construct a grant proposal that is persuasive and appealing to a reviewer.

MANAGING TIME WHEN WRITING

There are two aspects that lead to success in writing *and completing* the grant proposal. They consist of keeping yourself motivated and using effective time management. The ability to keep yourself motivated and achieve the goal of finishing a successful proposal is critical to your success. One of the best strategies to keep you motivated is to use the self-fulfilling prophecy. This concept states that a belief in an event or expectation can actually cause it to happen. Therefore, beliefs become reality.

If you are confident and realistic, you can keep yourself motivated in finishing a high-quality grant proposal. One of the ways to do this is to place high expectations on yourself that are realistic and to build confidence by encouraging yourself that you can do this and that you will be successful. In addition to building your own confidence, it is good to work with a team when completing the grant proposal. If you have a strong and positive team, where all the members give each other positive feedback and support, you can keep a highly motivated climate.

Your team members can reinforce the strengths of each other as well as support and help those with weaknesses. For example, if a team member has strong skills in financial management, he or she can take the lead in developing the budget, which can help create not only a motivated team but a synergistic and quality product.

The use of effective time management is also critical in completing the grant proposal in a timely manner. It is not unusual for grant writers to feel overwhelmed, especially when there are many other obligations. However, you must learn to control your time or time will control you. Learning to manage your time during the grant writing process is similar to trying to stick to a diet. To be successful you must first have a genuine desire and total commitment to succeed.

It is important to make decisive but accurate decisions in grant writing. None of us have the luxury of unlimited time, and using resources sparingly and productively will help in finishing your grant proposal.

Keep in mind that being productive versus being busy are two different things. Many times people feel as long as they are busy working on a proposal that they are effectively using their time. This may not be the case. You need to spend quality time that focuses on achieving the objective of your grant proposal and not be distracted by busy work that is of less importance.

Using a backward timeline is a simple process, whereby you identify which stages of the proposal need to be done by when and then create the time frame with tasks and due dates. Some of the time management strategies you can use include the following:

- Make a daily to-do list.
- Prioritize your activities by A, B, and C.
- Delegate certain parts of the proposal to others.
- Maximize every minute and develop a sense of urgency.
- Be decisive and complete activities only once.

An effective strategy to prioritize your activities is labeling the most important "A"; the next important, "B"; and "C" for the least important. Then, you should start with your As as most important and not the Cs, which are least important. Do not be afraid to delegate activities when you can.

As you might suspect, effective time management can be very rewarding, motivating, and beneficial in completing the grant proposal. By learning to apply some of these simple but powerful time management strategies, you can become a more successful grant writer. Try to avoid the use of hedging and jargon, lack of planning and editing, using the wrong tone, developing an unclear budget, and focusing on the problem versus the solution. Recognizing these common reasons for ineffective writing can help to ensure a strong, successful grant proposal.

The next and final chapter of the book outlines the process of reviewing and submitting the grant proposal, working with funders when a grant is awarded, and what to do if the application is rejected.

CHAPTER 5 NOTATIONS

1. Remember that writing succinctly and clearly are key to successful grant writing.
2. Try to identify your communication style.
3. Consider using a cue outline to organize your work.
4. Set a schedule for managing your time—even if it means writing a paragraph each day.
5. Recognize the ways in which you are most productive.

REFLECTION

You are a member of the grant writing department at a university. You have been asked to give a presentation to your faculty over-viewing the key strategies in writing a grant proposal. What would you list as the key characteristics in writing an effective grant proposal, and identify the major sections in a typical grant proposal. Finally, end your outline by providing some tips and strategies for keeping yourself motivated and using effective time management.

6

Encore

Beyond the Proposal

After days, weeks, or even months of working on an innovative and collaborative grant proposal, you are finally finished. In a quick review—or recap—you glance through the proposal to ensure you have the project statement and narrative, matching goals and objectives, a strong example of the need for funding, a literature review that supports your timeline, and a thoughtful evaluation plan that shows your understanding of how to effectively measure the success of your grant—both during and after funding has been awarded.

However, as they say in classical music—"it's not over until the fat lady sings." This is a common expression that represents the ending of a large-scale opera and with the protagonist singing a dramatic aria to emphasize the ending of the musical score (specifically dramatized in Richard Wagner's *Der Ring das Nebelungan* cycle).

Even after all the writing, editing, revising, rewriting, and finalizing of your proposal, it is truly "not over" until the proposal has been completely submitted to the potential funder. In many cases, the process of submitting the grant application can be very challenging. Government agencies often suggest that you dedicate a minimum of one week to ten days to set up an account, submit your application, and ensure that it was appropriately received by the funding agency.

Funders rarely allow for late submissions. Any request for a late submission needs various approvals and can be a challenging process. Extenuating circumstances that may surround a late submission usually require a detailed cover letter providing an explanation of why a submission was late and what the reasons were for the late application. In our experiences, it is typically best to submit an application on time, when possible, or to wait for the next submission and review cycle.

REVIEWING THE PROPOSAL

It has been many years since granting agencies allow for "snail mail" submissions. The online submission portals make grant review and award notices more efficient. It also allows funding agencies to screen and track applications as they are received. Since grant applications are almost always submitted online, why risk a computer failure, power outage, or a simple miscommunication between you and your laptop? Do not wait until the last minute. Before starting an online application for submission, double-check that you have accurately addressed and covered all the basic requirements for a grant application.

Prior to submitting the grant proposal application, you should complete a detailed and careful review of the document and any additional attachments. Figure 6.1 provides an example grant application review checklist.

You should examine the contents to ensure that it conforms to the standards of the application guidelines, starting with the transmittal letter to the appendix and supplementary materials. Make sure that all your files are labeled and in their final formats. The cover page should be clear and concise; the title typically includes the "who," "what," and "where" of the proposal. Good titles are often limited to fifteen words and are written succinctly but descriptively.

In addition to the typical components of the grant proposal, a description of the institution is often required. Make sure that the history and mission of your institution are described either in a narrative form or within the grant application guidelines. Sometimes, this information is limited to the fiscal health or information on prior activities. These details are often filled into a preexisting form.

Many institutions also have a vision statement, which essentially consists of a narrative of the history and the goals of the institution. In many cases it is useful to include organizational charts, resumes of key grant recipients, lists of previous grants, and other organizational documents that will support the proposal. This demonstrates a strong awareness of having received grants and knowing how to successfully manage grants within your organization.

It is often useful to include other resources within the institution that can help support the process. Examples might include volunteers, strategic partnerships, associations with other institutions, and special equipment and supplies. The application is also a good avenue to list the

Section	Checklist
Transmittal Letter	✓Does it follow grant proposal guidelines? ✓Is it complete and error-free? ✓Is it clear, concise, and comprehensive?
Summary Page	✓Is it succinct and does it conform to proposal guidelines? ✓Does it state the goals, problem, scope, and budget?
Table of Contents	✓Are the headings consistent with text? ✓Is the spacing accurate and uniform ✓Are the page numbers correct?
Introduction	✓Is the background comprehensive? ✓Is there a clear statement of the problem? ✓Are the contents and terms clear? ✓Is it well organized?
The Need, Goals, and Objectives	✓Does it contain supporting sources? ✓Is the information current? ✓Are the goals and needs clear? ✓Are the objectives, benefits, and results defined?
Project Scope	✓Are the timeline and resources clearly defined? ✓Are the procedures and method clear? ✓Are the statistics and data clear? ✓Are the tables and figures clear and well presented?
Project Evaluation	✓Are the evaluation methods clearly explained? ✓Are all tools and assessments defined? ✓Is the cost benefit explained, if needed?
Budget Plan	✓Are salaries, supplies, equipment, travel, etc. listed? ✓Is the method of spending funds explained? ✓Is the overall budget detailed and accurate?
Future Funding	✓ Are continuing funding sources listed and explained? ✓Are all resources and funding listed and accurate?
Appendix	✓Are there sufficient references? ✓Do references follow appropriate style? ✓Is the manuscript formatted to proposal guidelines?

Figure 6.1. Grant Application Review Checklist

institution's past grants and awards. This will provide extra credibility for the institution or organization and help in the evaluation of the proposal.

FINDING FEEDBACK

When we need someone to read our paper, article, book, or grant proposal, our first instinct is to turn to an individual close to us. While this is often convenient and comfortable, try also to find someone who has successfully submitted and been awarded grants. This individual should preferably have some knowledge of grant writing or experience in submitting a grant, to be able to give appropriate feedback on what are the strengths and challenges of your proposal.

Make sure that your grant application has also been reviewed by all the co-authors or co-principal investigators. Allow time for feedback, additional discussions, meetings, or conference calls to discuss any changes or additions that need to be made. Ask for colleagues and peers to give feedback and suggestions to strengthen your overall ideas. However, asking people who were not directly involved with writing the proposal can offer a more objective review of the document. Never assume that the grant application is complete even when you think it is done.

Create a plan for reviewing and submitting the application. This timeline will help you determine when you need feedback from your colleagues and when to have final edits in place. Allow opportunity for follow-up with the program officer. It is generally appropriate to provide colleagues with at least two weeks for review and feedback. Recall also that granting agencies, particularly government grants, suggest at least ten days just for completing the online submission process. Ideally, you would *begin* the online application at least four weeks prior to the deadline.

Do not forget about the obvious points to the proposal, such as ensuring that correct numbers have been assigned to pages, there are adequate page breaks inserted, footnotes have been provided where needed, and all visuals (especially computer screen shots) are visible. It is not uncommon for documents that are sent via the Internet to lose quality or become unreadable due to technical transmission.

When possible, it is good to test the transmission of the document prior to sending the final submission. Many institutions have a formal department that can assist in the grant writing process. This department can be very valuable in ensuring the use of proper institutional format and consistent information as well as providing assistance in reviewing the document prior to submission.

Step 1	• Review application and complete checklist.
Step 2	• Send application to colleagues for feedback.
Step 3	• Finalize application.
Step 4	• Begin online submission several weeks before grant submission deadline.
Step 5	• Confirm contact information for Co-PIs, consultants, and assistants.
Step 6	• Gather information on university overhead or EID numbers.
Step 7	• Plan at least one week to complete the submission process.
Step 8	• Set a deadline for submission at least 10 days prior to grant deadline.
Step 9	• Contact program officer to confirm receipt or follow up with questions.

Figure 6.2. Grant Application Submission and Review Timeline

If such a department does not exist, try to reach out to a program officer with questions or concerns. Since you may have already established an earlier relationship with the program officer, you can use this conversation to inquire about portions of the online submission that may require additional attention.

IMPLEMENTING A SWOT ANALYSIS

A common and valuable tool for evaluating the proposal is to use a self-reflection SWOT analysis. SWOT stands for Strengths, Weaknesses, Opportunities, and Threats. Figure 6.3 illustrates an example of a grant proposal SWOT analysis. In completing the self-reflection of the proposal, an evaluation team should be assembled to review the grant proposal.

This process allows the team to identify strengths and general areas in need of improvement and to make corrections prior to submission of the grant proposal. For example, typical strengths might include a good introduction and summary and problem statement, but upon close

Grant Proposal SWOT Analysis

Directions: *Review your grant proposal and application and complete the strengths, weaknesses, opportunities, and threats below. Then prepare an action plan for improvement.*

(S) Strengths - Excellent introduction and summary - Well-defined problem statement - Good project evaluation plan - Excellent detailed budget plan	(W) Weaknesses - Did not follow guidelines - Did not include timeline - Lacked clear charts - Lacked clear solutions
(O) Opportunities - Other similar grant sources - Topic is in great need - Strong internal support - Creative approach to problem	(T) Threats - Many other potential submissions - Lack of funding - Attrition of team members - Internal conflicts of team members

Action Plan: *Develop an action plan based on the SWOT analysis for resubmitting the grant proposal or similar one for the future.*

Strengths: ____________________

Weaknesses: ____________________

Opportunities: ____________________

Threats: ____________________

Figure 6.3. Example of a Grant Proposal SWOT Analysis

evaluation, some weaknesses may be the lack of a thorough budget or clear solutions to the problem.

These two categories of strengths and weaknesses allow the reviewer to then improve upon strengths and make corrections. The third section, called opportunities, allows the reviewers to conduct benchmarking. Benchmarking is a method whereby other grant proposals that meet outstanding criteria are examined and compared to your grant proposal. Examining similar grant sources and proposals may yield additional ideas for creative and useful writing.

The last section of the SWOT analysis consists of "threats." This section allows you to examine some of the internal and external factors that may contribute to an unsuccessful proposal. Examples might include the lack of previous grant awards, strong competition, lack of sufficient grant funding agencies, as well as poor internal institutional support.

Once all four components of the SWOT analysis have been completed, a careful analysis should be done and then action plans established. These action plans consist of ways in which to improve the proposal that will lead to a higher probability of success.

Likewise, the SWOT analysis can be an effective tool to use after a grant rejection. Even though a grant proposal has been rejected, that does not mean the end of the proposal. Generally after analysis and improvements, the grant can be resubmitted to other sources. Also, it is possible that you may be able to resubmit the proposal at the next funding cycle. Priorities change at funding agencies—a proposal that was rejected at one cycle may be of more value or importance at a consecutive deadline.

The second technique in reviewing the grant proposal is to conduct a presentation. When you are able to present the grant proposal orally to a group of people, it allows you as well as the listeners to better evaluate the proposal. In other words, one of the best ways to ensure that you understand and have written a good proposal is when you are able to explain it. In some cases, grant sources require an oral presentation to a group of program officers or members of the funding board.

When reviewing the grant proposal through a presentation, think of it as a typical technical presentation consisting of these stages: the opening, the delivery, and the closing. In other words, think of the three stages as "tell them what you're going to tell them," "tell them," and then "tell them what you said." This provides a very sequential and logical approach to the proposal.

In the first stage, the opening, you should quickly engage the audience, provide an overview, statement of the problem, objectives, proposed solution, budget, and future funding. You do not need to go into details in each of these areas, but you need to explain that each of them will be covered. The opening should include introduction of the institution and grant proposal members.

Always provide good transitions between each topics. A transition shows your ability to write and communicate in a smooth manner from one topic to another. This creates a logical sequence that is easily understood by the readers or participants. Once you have transitioned into the delivery stage, a detailed review of the main topics of the proposal should be completed.

The delivery stage is a good opportunity to identify questions that might arise concerning the proposal. One of the most important parts of the delivery is the budget. A detailed and thorough coverage of the budget should be done.

The last part of the proposal presentation is the closing. The closing must have a natural ending that brings attention to the main points of the proposal. The closing reconfirms the statement of the problem, objectives, and costs and benefits. The scheduled time frame should be covered as well as future funding sources of the proposal. After the closing, an analysis of the proposal presentation can reveal many worthwhile opportunities for improvement.

SUBMITTING THE PROPOSAL

Earlier in this chapter, we suggested that you *begin* the online application at least four weeks prior to the deadline. Recall that Grants.gov suggests allocating at least five days for the submission process. After a complete review of the proposal, we suggest you should plan to *submit* the application at least ten days prior to the deadline.

For example, if a grant deadline is December 30, you should have started the application process by November 30, and then plan to submit all the materials by December 20. This will allow you extra time to prepare for any last-minute changes and save the heartache of missing a deadline.

Keep in mind that to continue building positive relationships with funding sources and program officers, a letter of appreciation should always be extended regardless of the outcome. While we mentioned the importance of building collaborations with program officers earlier (see chapter 2), these relationships become increasingly important as you prepare to submit your application. As you begin the submission process, you will find that you have numerous questions, ranging from identifying the fiscal health of your organization to including the supplementary materials.

If you have not reached out to a program officer yet, it is a good idea to send a quick email or pick up the phone and call the individual managing the award. Use this opportunity to ask any questions you have about the submission and review cycle.

Make sure to double-check the online application before submitting the final document. Prior to submission, ensure that all attachments are appropriately included and that these documents are the final versions (not the drafts). Include any other co-investigators in this review process. Every extra set of eyes helps to check for errors or missing information. Sometimes, it is helpful if the PI and Co-PI upload the files together. We have often found that in these last moments of submitting the grant, small questions are bound to arise.

Once the proposal is submitted, you should typically receive an email or confirmation page showing that the proposal was accepted. If you have not received such a confirmation, you should email the program officer and let them know that you submitted the grant and want to ensure that is appropriately documented. Program officers will typically reply within twenty-four hours indicating that the application was received or providing you with assistance in submitting your files correctly. Giving yourself enough time for potential errors will ensure that your application is appropriately accepted.

NEXT STEPS

After you have submitted the proposal, it is often a huge sigh of relief that this immense task is complete. But nothing is guaranteed—how will you know if you were awarded the grant and when will you find out?

The grant review cycle typically takes three to six months for the application to be reviewed and given feedback or recommendations for further steps. For government grants, this process could be longer, sometimes taking nearly nine months for feedback. A funder's website will list the review time, the review process, and the individuals involved with the application review and selection. Smaller foundations or local agencies tend to respond more quickly. If the funder is interested, they may reach out to you for further information or simply email with a notice of whether funding was awarded.

However, it is important to be cognizant that this is a waiting process. Continually reaching out to program officers may tarnish any positive future relationships. Remember that they want to fund projects as much as you want to find funding. As you wait, you may consider looking ahead to additional RFPs, upcoming cycles, or other granting agencies that may be able to fund similar projects.

Many larger agencies have different RFPs available during each funding cycle. So, even if you have submitted a grant now, you can submit another idea for a different project in a few months. Since each grant is reviewed independently of one another, you will not be competing for your own awards. You can even submit the same grant to different funders. Plan ahead and find ways to modify your proposal in the event of a rejection. Then you are not relegated to waiting several months or a year before submitting a proposal to another cycle. You can immediately submit the proposal to another funding agency.

THE REVIEWERS

Every funding agency also has a board or panel that will review your proposal and ultimately make a decision on whether the grant should be funded. It is important for you to know who will be reading your proposal. Familiarize yourself with the review process. In a traditional peer review setting, the panel is chosen from a list of scholars in a field related to the discipline in which you are applying. For example, the reviewers for government agencies such as NIH and NEA are all expert scholars in their respective fields (e.g., health studies, music education).

Alternatively, many private foundations have panelists and reviewers who are not experts in their field, but represent the views, goals, and missions of the foundation itself. In this setting, the reviewers are charged with finding proposals that make a good match for the foundation's donation goals, rather than those that are simply a good fit within a discipline or field of study. The reviewers may simply be the program officers paging through LOIs or executive summaries, or they could be a group of individuals tasked with selecting a few proposals to share with the executive board.

In this instance, it is even more important to consider who will be reading the proposal. If you used abbreviations, acronyms, or discipline-specific terms that may not be understood outside of your field of study, explain these in more detail within your proposal or consider including a short list of definitions and a glossary of terms.

For example, the software program *Finale* is a common tool used to teach composition in music classrooms. If a classroom teacher were to apply for funding to build an instrumental music program and described how students would use *Finale*, reviewers who did not have a music background would not have any idea what *Finale* is or how it would be used.

Spend time double-checking any terms, programs, or tools that may be discipline specific. When in doubt, include descriptions of all the major terms used in the proposal in a separate document and direct your readers to this document in your narrative. This is a good way to further utilize supplementary materials and additional files to support your proposal. If your project is very focused within your discipline, it becomes even more important to solicit the help of an "outside reviewer" to provide feedback and suggestions on clarity in your proposal.

AFTER THE SUBMISSION

After the grant proposal has been successfully submitted, there are three responses that you could receive from the funding agency. The first, and most desirable, is yes—your proposal was funded. You will typically receive an email or confirmation letter stating that you were awarded the grant and listing any important next steps.

Amidst celebrations, it is important that you reach out to the program officer and thank him or her for the award and information. This is the time to also confirm with the program officer that there are no immediate changes being made to the award since your proposal was submitted. These changes could be internal (from the funder) or external (your own setting). Any changes in time or effort from you, personnel involved, the focus of the grant (sample population), or length of time should be reviewed and addressed.

Additionally, document any information that will be required for reporting the outcomes of your grant. Some agencies have specific formats or outlines that need to be included in your final reports. Make sure that you know exactly what will need to be reported and the format for reporting your grant award so that you can address the contents as you manage your award. In other words, plan ahead.

Once you have confirmed the receipt of the award, work with the indi viduals within your university or organization who will help to manage funds to ensure that the grant monies are distributed efficiently. Many universities have an office of sponsored research and programs that helps manage the funding. This office will have specific requirements for the grantee, such as completing conflict-of-interest training and disclosure statements.

Similarly, it is necessary to have a meeting with your collaborative team to discuss the implementation and organization of the award. Since you spent so much time planning and writing the proposal, budget, timeline, and assessment, this process should go seamlessly. Reiterate everyone's responsibilities—the steps for distributing funds, implementing the project, follow-up, and assessment. This is a good time to review your proposal and address any changes that may arise.

As you work through the process of managing your award, keep your program officer aware of any changes or information that may impact the outcome of your final report. Funders want to be involved with the money they distributed. Reach out to program officers and provide updates or interim reports on your progress. This way there are no surprises at the end, and the funder will appreciate your responsiveness.

LOOKING FORWARD

If you did not immediately receive a "yes" for your proposal, don't despair; some agencies reach out to PIs requesting more information. This is a good sign as it shows interest in your ideas. Make sure to find out *exactly* what is needed so that a full review of your proposal can be completed. Sometimes the reviewers will give specific suggestions of changes to make. These suggestions could include modifying the budget (the most common change suggested in grant proposal revisions), expanding the description of major project activities, or providing additional information on personnel involved with the grant.

Additionally, submit the revisions to the appropriate online portal and meet the deadline. Many times if you miss a deadline for revision, the grant will be rejected and considered as a new application for a different cycle. Take note of the revisions asked for so that even if the grant is rejected after a revision, you are more aware of what this particular funder wanted. It is also an opportunity to identify your own strengths and weaknesses within grant writing.

Finally, the last outcome is that your proposal could be rejected. While this is obviously disheartening, do not see this as the end of your proposal. Consider how many articles you have written that may have been similarly rejected. One piece of advice we are always given is to revise the article and submit it to another journal. This process applies to grant writing as well.

If your proposal is rejected, contact the program officer and ask if there is any way to receive feedback on what was missing or was not a good fit. Very often the program officers are willing to spend time to talk with you on the phone to discuss how to strengthen your proposal. You can then use this information to reapply another time, for another grant, or to seek a different funding agency with the same proposal. Consider the following three steps after a rejected proposal:

1. Contact the program officer and thank him or her for reviewing the proposal.
2. Ask for detailed feedback on why the proposal was rejected, if it was not a good fit, did not align with current initiatives, or any other specific concerns from the funder's perspective.

3. Find other RFPs within the current funding agency or modify the proposal and submit elsewhere.

Remember that grant applications are not like scholarly articles. There is no requirement that a proposal has to be exclusively submitted somewhere. You can seek funding for the same project at many different places. The only challenge is to ensure that you are tailoring your proposal to all the needs and requirements of each, individual request for proposals.

Ask the program officer if there are other, similar grants that might be a stronger fit for your proposal since you were not awarded funds. And make sure to follow up with a thank-you letter. In our digital age, a handwritten note can provide a stronger response than an email.

Through the various steps of locating funding agencies, selecting an RFP, reaching out to program officers, collaborating with colleagues, building a grant writing team, and revising and editing your work, we hope that you will come to understand and appreciate the ebbs and flows of grant writing. Even if you are not awarded a grant the first time you apply, the processes we have outlined throughout this book will hopefully guide you in revising and resubmitting your proposal to other funders.

Grant writing is not only an opportunity to gather external funding but also a venue to build and foster meaningful professional relationships both within your organization and among program officers. There is money to be awarded. It just takes time, perseverance, and utilization of the various strategies needed for writing successful grant proposals.

CHAPTER 6 NOTATIONS

1. Plan ahead to submit your proposal—allocate at least one week for online submissions.
2. Invite colleagues to read through your proposal and application and give feedback.
3. Familiarize yourself with the review process for the funding agency you are contacting.
4. Reach out to the program officer regardless of the outcome of your proposal.
5. If your proposal is rejected, consider minor revisions and resubmit to another funder.

REFLECTION

If you could receive funding for any project, idea, collaboration, research, or initiative that you want, what would you choose? Who are your strongest collaborators? Can you justify the need for support? Which areas are strong and which are weak?

Da Capo

Epilogue

Many people wonder if grant writing is worth the effort. While some scholars are not necessarily required to write grants or seek external funding, other professionals, faculty positions, or organizations are often reliant upon grants to support ongoing research and projects.

In music, *da capo* is literally defined as "the head" in Italian and means a return to the beginning. The grant writing process is cyclical in many ways—you start with an idea that you hope to get funded, research and collaborate with colleagues, try to pursue funding, and if funded, implement your idea and try to secure additional grants. If not, you seek funding elsewhere but return again to your research, teaching, consulting, and practice. You return back to the beginning.

The grant proposal itself holds a similar structure. If you recall, we discussed the importance of considering the end at the beginning—writing the evaluation as you describe the narrative. This cycle demonstrates how we are always returning back to where we started, recalling the main ideas, and reflecting on our directions.

Consider your own situation within this larger context. What does grant writing mean to you or more importantly, what does it mean *for* you? Do you feel more connected with smaller, local agencies, or are you seeking the opportunity to travel abroad through a large, grant-funded project? Do you *need* grants, or do you want grants?

As the field of grant writing continues to shift, change, and evolve into a discipline that is valued, challenged, recognized, and submerged within other fields, it is important to evaluate how your own views of grant seeking influence your experience with writing grants.

The ideas, outlines, figures, tables, suggestions, questions, and thoughts that we have presented in this book are meant to be as such—guidelines for framing your own research questions, delving into possibilities that only you can imagine, and finding ways to advocate, support, and promote the work you are already doing.

Ultimately, just as we will always need teachers, scholars, artists, doctors, engineers, mathematicians, and those fields that continue to shape our society, so too will we also need grants. These awards are two-fold: First, being awarded a grant means that you will have external funds to support the research you are already invested in within your own practice. Grant writing is an intersection between the fields of research and practice. The projects we implement in our classrooms and communities can be documented and promoted through research, and supported through grants.

Finally, and perhaps more important, receiving a grant brings with it a sense of validation, prestige, and accomplishment. Maybe you do not necessarily need a grant to support your work, but let us all be honest, a little money can go a long way.

Appendix A

GRANT PROFESSIONALS ASSOCIATION CODE OF ETHICS AND STANDARDS

Members, among others, are to:

- Practice their profession with the highest sense of integrity, honesty, and truthfulness to maintain and broaden public confidence
- Adhere to all applicable laws and regulations in all aspects of grantsmanship
- Continually improve their professional knowledge and skills
- Promote positive relationships between grant professionals and their stakeholders
- Value the privacy, freedom, choice and interests of all those affected by their actions
- Ensure that funds are solicited according to program guidelines
- Adhere to acceptable means of compensation for services performed; pro bono work is encouraged
- Foster cultural diversity and pluralistic values and treat all people with dignity and respect
- Become leaders and role models in the field of grantsmanship
- Encourage colleagues to embrace and practice GPA's Code of Ethics and Standards of Professional Practice.

STANDARDS OF PROFESSIONAL PRACTICE

As members respect and honor the above principles and guidelines established by the GPA Code of Ethics, any infringement or breach of standards outlined in the Code are subject to disciplinary sanctions, including expulsion, to be determined by a committee elected by their peers.

PROFESSIONAL OBLIGATIONS

1. Members shall act according to the highest ethical standards of their institution, profession, and conscience.
2. Members shall obey all applicable local, state, provincial, and federal civil and criminal laws and regulations.
3. Members shall avoid the appearance of any criminal offense or professional misconduct.
4. Members shall disclose all relationships that might constitute, or appear to constitute, conflicts of interest.
5. Members shall not be associated directly or indirectly with any service, product, individuals, or organizations in a way that they know is misleading.
6. Members shall not abuse any relationship with a donor, prospect, volunteer or employee to the benefit of the member or the member's organization.
7. Members shall recognize their individual boundaries of competence and are forthcoming and truthful about their professional experience, knowledge and expertise.
8. Members shall continually strive to improve their personal competence.

Source: Grant Professionals Association, 2014

Appendix B

GRANT PUBLIC LAW 106-107

The Grants Policy Committee (GPC), a committee of the U.S. Chief Financial Officers Council, has responsibility for coordinating government-wide streamlining and simplification activities for federal grants and cooperative agreements. The GPC recommends financial assistance policies and practices to the Office of Management and Budget and coordinates related interagency activities.

The GPC's improvement efforts gained significant momentum when the committee assumed responsibility for coordinating government-wide implementation of P.L. 106-107, the Federal Financial Management Assistance Act of 1999, which had improving the effectiveness of federal financial assistance programs, coordination and streamlining as its primary goals. While P.L. 106-107 expired in November 2007, the GPC continues to build on this momentum, advancing existing efforts and leveraging new opportunities to enhance federal financial assistance.

The GPC continues its interagency coordination and its recommendations to OMB, serving the public interest in collaboration with other federal-wide grants initiatives.

Grants.gov was created to provide a single website for all federal grant opportunities. It was called for from the President's Management Agenda and also as part of the Public Law 106-107, which is to streamline and simplify the way the federal government does grants. It simplifies the grants management process by providing a central online system to find and apply for grants across the federal government.

When you receive a grant or cooperative agreement award, it lists general terms and conditions, such as Office of Management and Budget Circulars, agency regulations implementing government-wide requirements. Currently you can find the OMB requirements on OMB's home page, and may be able to find the agency's regulations at the agency's website or by a search of the Code of Federal Regulations (CFR). Recently OMB established a new Title 2 in the CFR as part of government-wide streamlining activities. The plan for Title 2 is to enable you to find all OMB Circulars and guidance to the agencies and the agency regulations implementing them in that single title. This will be accomplished over the next several years as the streamlining progresses.

The statutory language of P.L. 106-107 addressed financial assistance in general, which would have included loans, loan guarantees, and other forms of financial assistance. However, government-wide streamlining activities have focused on financial assistance in the form of grants and cooperative agreements, where the twenty-six grant-making agencies believe there is the greatest opportunity to streamline and simplify. Grants and cooperative agreements are awarded to all sectors—public and private, nonprofit and for-profit—and account for billions of dollars and millions of transactions. Although programs differ, these award instruments generally are subject to the same government-wide regulatory and policy framework.

Grants.gov FIND provides "one-stop shopping" that will allow you to review synopses of all available competing funding opportunities for grants and cooperative agreements (and other types of financial assistance if the funding agency chooses) under the hundreds of discretionary grant programs. You can search by agency, category of activity to be funded, Catalog of Federal Domestic Assistance number, and other parameters. You also can sign up for email notification of newly posted opportunities based on parameters it provides.

Source: Grants.gov

Appendix C

GRANTS.GOV PRIVACY POLICY

Grants.gov privacy policy protects the rights of individual users under section 552a of title 5, United States Code (commonly referred to as the 'Privacy Act,' and other laws relevant to the protection of the privacy of an individual). All information is gathered, stored, and used in accordance with the above-mentioned Privacy Act.

Our privacy and security policy is clear: *We will collect no personal information about you when you visit our website unless you choose to provide that information to us.*

Information Collected and Stored Automatically

Grants.gov does not require a user to submit information to browse the Grants.gov site. The only users who are required to submit contact information are those users who wish to be authorized submitters on behalf of their organization, or users who wish to receive information directly from Grants.gov.

Grants.gov collects personal information about you (e.g., name, email address, phone number, title, username) only if you specifically and knowingly give it to us. If you consent to provide us with personal information (by providing feedback or by asking a question), we use that information to respond to your message and to help us get you the information you have requested. We only share the information you give us with other government agencies if your inquiry relates to that agency, or as otherwise required by law. Moreover, we do not create individual profiles with the information you provide or give it to any private organizations. We do not collect information for commercial marketing.

Grants.gov collects information to allow access for three types of users:

- Agency Users
- Authorized Organization Representatives

All information collected and stored is in compliance with the Paperwork Reduction Act. Any information submitted to Grants.gov through the application process will be stored in the Grants.gov system for a period of six months. Additionally, no one from Grants.gov will ever ask you for personal information, such as your Social Security number, banking, or credit card information.

When you browse, read pages or download information on Grants.gov, we automatically gather and store certain technical information about your visit. This information never identifies who you are. The information we collect and store about your visit is listed below:

- The Internet domain (e.g., "xcompany.com" if you use a private Internet access account, or "yourschool.edu" if you connect from a university's domain) and IP address (an IP address is a number that is automatically assigned to your computer whenever you are surfing the Web) from which you access our website;
- The type of browser (e.g., Netscape, Internet Explorer) and operating system (e.g., Windows, Unix) used to access our website;
- The date and time you access our website;
- The pages you visit; and
- If you linked to the Grants.gov website from another website, the address of the website.

This information is only used to help us make the site more useful for you. With this data we learn about the number of visitors to our site and the types of technology our visitors use. We never track or record information about individuals and their visits.

Site Security

For site security purposes and to ensure that this service remains available to all users, this government computer system is housed in a secure government facility and employs commercial software programs to monitor network traffic to identify unauthorized attempts to upload, view, change information, or otherwise cause damage.

Except for authorized law enforcement investigations, no other attempts are made to identify individual users or their usage habits. Unauthorized attempts to upload, view, or change information on this site are strictly prohibited and may be punishable under the Computer Fraud and Abuse Act of 1986 and the National Information Infrastructure Protection Act.

Links to Other Sites

This website has links to other websites. Once you link to another site, you are subject to the privacy policy of the new site. The Grants.gov link is provided as a public service only. These web pages are provided as a tool to help visitors explore the wide range of options and information available, and to help them make informed choices about how to prepare for and pursue grant application opportunities. As such, the organization, services, advice, or products are not endorsed or guaranteed in any way by Grants.gov and are entirely the responsibility of the sponsor of the site visited.

Cookies

To use this website, you must enable cookies support in your web browser. Cookies will only be used for the duration of the individual session to allow you easy navigation within the website. A cookie is a small piece of information that is sent to your browser, along with a webpage, when you access a website. There are two kinds of cookies. A session cookie is a line of text that is stored temporarily in your computer's RAM. Because a session cookie is never written to a drive, it is destroyed as soon as you close your browser. A persistent cookie is a more permanent line of text that gets saved by your browser to a file on your hard drive. Depending on your browser settings, you may receive notification that a given site is requesting cookie information, possibly with an expiration date. Persistent cookies have an expiration date in the future. Session cookies have no date associated with them. The Grants.gov website will create a session cookie whenever you access the website. The session cookie is automatically destroyed as soon as you close your browser. We do not create any persistent cookies.

Source: Grants.gov

Appendix D

ELIGIBILITY FOR GOVERNMENT GRANTS

There are many groups of organizations that are eligible to apply for government funding opportunities, posted on Grants.gov. Typically, most applicant organizations fall into the following categories.

Government Organizations

- State Governments
- Local Governments
- City or Township Governments
- Special District Governments
- Native American Tribal Governments (federally recognized)
- Native American Tribal Governments (other than federally recognized)

Education Organizations

- Independent School Districts
- Public and State-Controlled Institutions of Higher Education
- Private Institutions of Higher Education

Public Housing Organizations

- Public Housing Authorities
- Indian Housing Authorities

Nonprofit Organizations

- Nonprofits having a 501(c)(3) status with the IRS, other than institutions of higher education
- Nonprofits that do not have a 501(c)(3) status with the IRS, other than institutions of higher education

For-Profit Organizations (other than small businesses)

Small Businesses

Small business grants may be awarded to companies meeting the size standards that the U.S. Small Business Administration (SBA) has established for most industries in the economy. The most common size standards are as follows:

- 500 employees for most manufacturing and mining industries
- 100 employees for all wholesale trade industries
- $6 million for most retail and service industries
- $28.5 million for most general and heavy construction industries
- $12 million for all special trade contractors
- $0.75 million for most agricultural industries

Individuals

Individuals submit funding opportunity applications on their behalf, and not on behalf of a company, organization, institution, or government. If registered as an individual, you are only allowed to apply to funding opportunities that are open to individuals.

Source: Grants.gov

Appendix E

PROCESSES FOR GRANT APPLICATION

You will find more detailed information; navigate to our Get Registered page or the Applicants User Guide.

1. Obtain a DUNS number (optional for Individual applicants).
2. Register with SAM.gov (optional for Individual applicants). Organization Applicants will not be able to move on to Step #3 until this step is completed.
3. Create a Grants.gov username and password. You will need to create a Grants.gov user profile by visiting the Get Registered section of the website.
4. The E-Business Point of Contact (POC) at your organization must respond to the registration email from Grants.gov and login at Grants.gov to authorize you as an Authorized Organization Representative (AOR). Please note that there can be more than one AOR for an organization.
5. At any time, you can track your AOR status by going to the Applicant Login with your username and password.

Be sure to allow enough time to register prior to the submission deadline for your application package.

- Organization applicants with an Employer Identification Number (EIN) should allow seven business days to complete all five registration steps, but additional time may be required for AOR Authorization depending upon the responsiveness of your E-Biz POC.

- Organization applicants applying for an EIN should plan on a minimum of two full weeks but additional time may be required for AOR Authorization depending upon the responsiveness of your E-Biz POC.
- Individual applicants can register in as little as one business day.

Source: Grants.gov

Appendix F

SAMPLE GRANT REVIEW PROCESS
NATIONAL SCIENCE FOUNDATION

Phase I – Proposal Preparation and Submission (Ninety Days)

1. Opportunity Announced. All funding opportunities are announced on the NSF website and Grants.gov. Program Descriptions, Program Announcements and Program Solicitations are mechanisms used by NSF to generate proposals. Unsolicited proposals to specific NSF programs may be submitted at any time.
2. Proposal Submitted. The Grant Proposal Guide (GPG) is the source for guidance on preparing and submitting a proposal to NSF. The GPG details formatting and submission requirements. The proposing organization submits the proposal to NSF via the NSF FastLane System.
3. Proposal Received. Proposals are received by the NSF Proposal Processing Unit and are assigned to the appropriate program for acknowledgement and, if they meet NSF requirements, for review. A proposal may be returned without review if it does not meet NSF proposal preparation requirements, such as page limitations, formatting instructions, and electronic submission, as specified in the GPG or program solicitation. The GPG identifies all of the reasons for which a proposal may be returned without review.

Phase II – Proposal Review and Processing (Six Months)

4. Reviewers Selected. Reviewers are selected based on their specific and/or broad knowledge of the science and engineering fields; their broad knowledge of the infrastructure of the science and engineering enterprise, and its educational activities; and to the extent possible, diverse representation within the review group. Sources of reviewers can come from the program officer's knowledge of the research area; references listed in the proposal; recent professional society programs; computer searches of science and engineering journal articles related to the proposal; reviewer recommendations included in proposal or sent by email. Proposers are invited to suggest persons they believe are especially well qualified to review the proposal, as well as identify persons they would prefer not review the proposal.
5. Peer Review. All NSF proposals are reviewed through use of the two NSB-approved merit review criteria: Intellectual Merit and Broader Impacts. Some solicitations may have additional review criteria. External reviewers' analyses and evaluation of the proposal provide information to the NSF program officer in making a recommendation regarding the proposal.
6. Program Officer Recommendation. After scientific, technical, and programmatic review, the NSF program officer recommends to the cognizant division director whether the proposal should be recommended for an award or declined for funding. Due to the large number of proposals received, the review and consideration process can take up to six months. Large or particularly complex proposals may require additional review and processing time.
7. Division Director Review. If the decision is made to decline the award, the organization is notified and review information is available in the FastLane System. If the decision is to award, the recommendation is submitted to a Grants and Agreements officer in the Division of Grants and Agreements (DGA).

Phase III – Award Processing (Thirty Days)

8. Business Review. The Grants and Agreements officer in the Division of Grants and Agreements (DGA) conducts a review of business, financial, and policy implications. Generally, DGA makes awards within thirty days after the program office makes its recommendation. Additional processing time may be required if the organization has not received prior funding, if the award is a cooperative

agreement, or it involves special situations (such as coordination with another federal agency or a private funding source).

9. Award Finalized. The award itself is comprised of an award notice, budget, proposal, applicable NSF conditions, and any other documents or requirements incorporated by reference into the agreement. Each NSF award notice specifically identifies certain conditions that are applicable to, and become part of, that award.

Source: National Science Foundation

Appendix G

SAMPLE GRANT REVIEW PROCESS OF THE NATIONAL ENDOWMENT FOR THE HUMANITIES

1. Applicant submits applications package to Grants.gov by deadline.
2. NEH assembles peer-review panel. Knowledgeable persons outside NEH read each application and advise the agency about its merits.
3. Using peer-review evaluations, NEH staff recommends applications for funding based on available funds.
4. National Council on the Humanities, which meets three times a year, reviews the recommended applications.
5. NEH chairman takes into account the advice provided by the review process and, by law, makes all funding decisions.
6. Applicants are notified whether their projects will be funded.

Source: National Endowment for the Humanities

Appendix H

SAMPLE LETTER OF INTENT

Attn: Grants Agency
1234 Money Matters Avenue
Anywhere, USA 00000

Date

Dear Mr./Mrs. Program Officer,

I am writing with great interest to apply for the Grants Agency, Research for Scholars and Professionals Award for our project titled Music Rocks! We hope to continue the study of the interactions between professional musicians and concert attendees. This project is currently completing the first year of funding at Music University. Our preliminary findings suggest that there is a strong relationship between concert attendees' age, music listening skills, and at-home musical experiences when compared with the professional musicians' background and training.

Our project is led by a team of experts in the field who have researched this phenomenon for over five years. We all hold graduate degrees in our areas of expertise. This grant would support our plans to expand our sample population beyond one metropolitan area and would provide additional support for two graduate students who are involved with data collection and analysis.

Thank you for your time and consideration. We look forward to the opportunity to submit a full proposal.

Sincerely,

The Grant Writers
San Diego, CA

Appendix I

SAMPLE FINAL REPORT

Date

To: John Smith
Grant Director
Funding Agency
1400 Maple Tree Avenue
Hometown, IL 60000

RE: Project report for grant

Dear Mr. Smith:
We are pleased to provide this report on the Management and Security grant project.

Project Results: The Management and Security (MS) program was successfully developed. It is a web-based tool that can be used by organizations to test their management programs. The software program allows users to test their management plan through the use of scenarios and preprogrammed information such as additional mini-scenarios "injects."

Web Address: Here is the web address to try out the program: www.abcd.com

Program Features: Users can select from ten test conditions to assess their management plan:

1. Business Continuity Management
2. Management and Communication
3. Critical Infrastructure
4. Emergency Management
5. Facility Management
6. Legal Compliance and Audit
7. Organizational Behavior
8. Risk Management and Insurance
9. Social Resilience
10. Supply Chain Logistics and Transportation Management

- Contained in the MS software are prewritten scenarios that are used to test your management plan.
- The user has the ability to customize the scenario to suit the organization.
- Prewritten "injects" are contained to provide additional testing of the management plan.
- The program automatically saves the management scenario.
- The user has the ability to edit the introduction and conclusion scenarios.
- The user has the ability to log history and activity for saved scenarios such as date, attendees, notes, and action items.
- There is a "Print This Scenario" link that opens a printable version of the scenario.

Development Background: This program was developed by the Action consulting team and worked in a cross-functional team environment. Two multidisciplinary teams were used to engage the project development over a six-month period. The team had support from the Dynamic consulting team leader. This product has potential commercialization and could help solve the problem for many organizations. For additional information contact:

Grant Writers, PhD
Management Programs
Houston, TX

Future Projections/Milestones

This, originally planned as a multi-funded project, will incorporate these phases:

1. Development of the scenario template (methodology) and scenarios (completed)
2. Test the scenario template with social and private agencies (completed and additional testing will be performed)
3. Develop it into a web-based program that can be posted on the Internet and used by organizations (completed, and additional plans for web hosting are planned)
4. Further enhancement of the program and improved navigation and use.

Project Budget

The grant money ($50,000) used to support this program has been officially accounted and approved by the institution of grant services.

Sincerely,

Grant Writers, PhD
Management Programs
Houston, TX

Appendix J

GLOSSARY OF TERMS

Accrued Expenditures
Charges incurred by a recipient during a given period requiring the provision of funds for (1) goods and other tangible property received; (2) services performed by employees, contractors, subrecipients, and other payees; and (3) other amounts becoming owed under programs for which no current services or performance is required.

Accrued Income
Sum of (1) earnings during a given period from (a) services performed by the recipient, and (b) goods and other tangible property delivered to purchasers; and (2) amount becoming owed to the recipient for which no current services or performance is required by the recipient.

Acquisition Cost of Equipment
Net invoice price of the equipment, including the cost of modifications, attachments, accessories, or auxiliary apparatus necessary to make the property usable for the purpose for which it was acquired. Other charges, such as the cost of installation, transportation, taxes, duty, or protective in-transit insurance, shall be included or excluded from the unit acquisition cost in accordance with the recipient's regular accounting practices.

Adobe Reader
A free software that will allow you to access, complete, and submit application packages electronically and securely through Grants.gov. Please be sure you have the compatible version installed.

Advance Payment
A payment made to a recipient upon its request either before outlays are made by the recipient or through the use of predetermined payment schedules.
Agency Enrollment Code
A federal grantor agency identifier within the Grants.gov system; that links grantor users to their participating grantor agency and enables the grantor agency "Super User" status to assign rights and responsibilities to members of their agency. The agency enrollment code is required for grantor registration and is only given to members of a grantor agency responsible for managing opportunities, application review, generating reports, and other grantor functions at Grants.gov. This is *not* required for applicants applying for grants.
Agency-Specific Data Sets
Data that an agency collects in addition to data on any of the SF-424 series forms.
American Recovery and Reinvestment Act (ARRA) of 2009
The economic stimulus package of $787 billion (also known as the "Recovery Act") was signed into law by the president on February 17, 2009. "Making supplemental appropriations for job preservation and creation, infrastructure investment, energy efficiency and science, assistance to the unemployed, and State and local fiscal stabilization, for the fiscal year ending September 30, 2009, and for other purposes."
Application Package
A group of specific forms and documents for a specific funding opportunity which are used to apply for a grant.
Application Package Template
One or more forms and documents that can be reused for multiple opportunity-specific application packages.
ARRA
See American Recovery and Reinvestment Act of 2009.
Authorized Organization Representative (AOR)
An AOR submits a grant on behalf of a company, organization, institution, or government. Only an AOR has the authority to sign and submit grant applications.
Award
Financial assistance that provides support or stimulation to accomplish a public purpose. Awards include grants and other agreements in the form of money or property in lieu of money, by the federal government to an eligible recipient. The term does not include technical assistance, which provides services instead of money; other assistance in the form of loans, loan guarantees, interest subsidies, or insurance; direct payments of any

kind to individuals; and contracts that are required to be entered into and administered under federal procurement laws and regulations.

Benefits

A payment made or an entitlement available in accordance with a wage agreement, an insurance policy, or a public assistance program.

Benefits.gov

Federal website created by the White House in 2002 to provide citizens with easy online access to government benefit and assistance programs, established to launch and manage a diverse portfolio of government-to-citizen, government-to-business and government-to-government websites. Operated, managed, and supported by federal agency partnerships, these initiatives provide high-quality solutions such as citizen tax filing, federal rule making, electronic training, and benefit information delivery. The beneficiaries include citizens, businesses, and federal and state government employees.

Cage Code

A five-character code that identifies companies doing, or planning to do, business with the federal government and is assigned through the System for Award Management (SAM).

Cash Contributions

A recipient's cash outlay, including the outlay of money contributed to the recipient by third parties.

Catalog of Federal Domestic Assistance (CFDA)

An online database of all federal programs available to state and local governments; federally recognized Indian tribal governments; territories and possessions of the United States; domestic public, quasi-public, and private profit and nonprofit organizations; and institutions, specialized groups, and individuals.

Catalog of Federal Domestic Assistance (CFDA) Number

The identifying number that a federal program is assigned in the Catalog of Federal Domestic Assistance (CFDA).

Central Contractor Registration (CCR)

The Central Contractor Registry (CCR) was the primary vendor database for the U.S. federal government. CCR functionality was migrated to the System for Award Management (SAM) in late July 2012.

Close Date

The grantor agency designated deadline for submission of a particular grant application. See also Grace Period.

Closeout

Process by which the awarding agency determines that all applicable administrative actions and all required work of the award have been completed by the recipient and the awarding agency.

Competition ID
A grantor-selected ID that allows further distinction of the funding opportunity number that allows applications with the same funding opportunity number to be assigned unique identifiers.
Contract
A procurement contract under an award or subaward, and a procurement subcontract under a recipient's or sub-recipient's contract.
Congressional District
One of a fixed number of districts into which a state is divided, each district electing one member to the national House of Representatives.
Cooperative Agreement
An award of financial assistance that is used to enter into the same kind of relationship as a grant; it is distinguished from a grant in that it provides for substantial involvement between the federal agency and the recipient in carrying out the activity contemplated by the award.
Cost Sharing or Matching
The portion of project or program costs not borne by the federal government.
Current Accounting Period
The period of time the recipient chooses for purposes of financial statements and audits.
Data Universal Numbering System (DUNS)
A unique nine-character identification number provided by the commercial company Dun & Bradstreet (D&B).
Date of Completion
The date on which all work under an award is completed or the date on the award document or any supplement or amendment thereto, on which awarding agency sponsorship ends.
Disallowed Costs
Charges to an award that the awarding agency determines to be unallowable, in accordance with the applicable federal cost principles or other terms and conditions contained in the award.
Discretionary Grant
A grant (or cooperative agreement) for which the federal awarding agency generally may select the recipient from among all eligible recipients, may decide to make or not make an award based on the programmatic, technical, or scientific content of an application, and can decide the amount of funding to be awarded.
Download
Transferring data (usually a file) from another computer to the computer you are using.

Earmark Grants

Earmark grants are grants that are appropriated by Congress prior to a peer review. The term "earmark" is a reference to the Congressional Record where the awards are written into the legislation specifically with the grant applicant's name, activity, and dollar amounts.

E-Business Point of Contact (E-Biz POC)

An E-Business Point of Contact is responsible for the administration and management of grant activities in his or her organization. The E-Biz POC authorizes representatives of their organization (see Authorized Organization Representative [AOR]) to submit grant applications through Grants.gov. An E-Biz POC must also register as an AOR to submit an application.

E-Gov

Office of E-Government & Information Technology (E-Gov) is a part of the Office of Management and Budget (OMB) electronic government initiative. Created in an effort to use technology to provide and improve government services, transactions, and interactions with citizens, businesses, and other arms of government.

Entitlements

A government program that guarantees and provides benefits to a particular group.

Equipment

Tangible nonexpendable personal property, including exempt property, charged directly to the award and having a useful life of more than one year and an acquisition cost of $5,000 or more per unit. However, consistent with recipient policy, lower limits may be established.

Excess Property

Property under the control of an awarding agency that, as determined by the head of the awarding agency or his/her delegate, is no longer required for the agency's needs or the discharge of its responsibilities.

Exempt Property

Tangible personal property acquired in whole or in part with federal funds, where the awarding agency has statutory authority to vest title in the recipient without further obligation to the federal government. An example of exempt property authority is contained in the federal Grant and Cooperative Agreement Act, 31 U.S.C. 6306, for property acquired under an award to conduct basic or applied research by a nonprofit institution of higher education or nonprofit organization whose principal purpose is conducting scientific research.

FedBizOpps.gov

Single point of entry for commercial vendors and government buyers to post, search, monitor, and retrieve opportunities solicited by the entire federal contracting community.

Federal Share of Real Property, Equipment, or Supplies
The percentage of the properties or supplies acquisition costs and any improvement expenditures paid with federal funds. This will be the same percentage as the federal share of the total costs under the award for the funding period in which the property was acquired (excluding the value of third-party, in-kind contributions).
Federally Recognized Indian Tribal Government
The governing body of any Indian tribe, band, nation, or other organized group or community (including any Native village as defined in section 3 of the Alaska Native Claims Settlement Act certified by the Secretary of the Interior as eligible for the special programs and services provided by him through the Bureau of Indian Affairs).
Fedgrants.gov
A website that has been shut down. When it was live, its purpose was to enable users to search for grant opportunities.
Financial Assistance
The transfer of a thing of value from a federal agency to a recipient to carry out a public purpose of support or stimulation authorized by a law of the United States (see 31 U.S.C. 6101(3)). An agency may provide financial assistance through various types of transactions, including grants, cooperative agreements, loans, loan guarantees, interest subsidies, insurance, food commodities, direct appropriations, and transfers of property in place of money.
Funding Opportunity Announcement
A publicly available document by which a federal agency makes known its intentions to award discretionary grants or cooperative agreements, usually as a result of competition for funds. Funding opportunity announcements may be known as program announcements, notices of funding availability, solicitations, or other names depending on the agency and type of program. Funding opportunity announcements can be found at Grants.gov/FIND and on the Internet at the funding agency's or program's website.
Funding Opportunity Number
The number that a federal agency assigns to its grant announcement.
Funding Period
The period of time when federal funding is available for obligation by the recipient.
Government
A state or local government or a federally recognized Indian tribal government.
Grace Period
A grace period may be created at the grantor agency's discretion to extend the application submission period. This period reflects the number

of days after the closing date that Grants.gov will continue to accept applications for a grant opportunity, for example, an agency might include a grace period to accept revised applications. It also represents the day (Closing Date + Grace Period) that applicants will no longer be able to download the application package. This value is entered by an agency when creating a grant opportunity and is not visible to grant applicants.

Grant

An award of financial assistance, the principal purpose of which is to transfer a thing of value from a federal agency to a recipient to carry out a public purpose of support or stimulation authorized by a law of the United States (see 31 U.S.C. 6101(3)). A grant is distinguished from a contract, which is used to acquire property or services for the federal government's direct benefit or use.

Grants.gov

A storefront web portal for use in electronic collection of data (forms and reports) for federal grant-making agencies through the Grants.gov site.

Grants.gov Tracking Number

A number set used by Grants.gov that is used to identify each application it receives.

Individual

An individual submits a grant on their behalf, and not on behalf of a company, organization, institution, or government. Individuals sign the grant application and its associated certifications and assurances that are necessary to fulfill the requirements of the application process.

Intangible Property and Debt Instruments

Includes trademarks, copyrights, patents, and patent applications, and such property as loans, notes and other debt instruments, lease agreements, stock, and other instruments of property ownership, whether considered tangible or intangible.

Inter-Agency Electronic Grants Committee (IAEGC)

An organization that encourages and assists federal agencies in developing electronic grants systems and standardizing electronic commerce methodologies throughout the federal government. The IAEGC is chartered to Grants.Gov Program Management Office.

Local Government

A local unit of government, including specifically a county, municipality, city, town, township, local public authority, school district, special district, intra-state district, council of governments (whether or not incorporated as a nonprofit corporation under state law), any other regional or interstate entity, or any agency or instrumentality of local government.

Login

The act of connecting to a computer system by giving your credentials (usually your "username" and "password").

Mandatory Forms
Mandatory forms are the forms that are required for the application. Please note that a mandatory form must be completed before the system will allow the applicant to submit the application package.
Mandatory Grant
A grant (or cooperative agreement) awarded under a program where the authorizing statute requires the head of the agency or designee to make an award to each eligible entity under the conditions and in the amount (or based on the formula) specified in the statute.
Marketing Partner ID (MPIN)
A personal code that allows you to access other government applications such as the Past Performance Automated System, DoDBusOpps, and TeDS. The MPIN may act as your password in these other systems. You make up the code and register it in SAM. The MPIN must have nine digits containing at least one alpha character (must be in capital letters) and one number (no spaces or special characters permitted).
North American Industry Classification System (NAICS) Code
A code with a maximum of six digits used to classify business establishments. This code will be replacing the Standard Industrial Classification (SIC) code.
Obligations
The amounts of orders placed, contracts and grants awarded, services received, and similar transactions during a given period that require payment by the recipient during the same or a future period.
Opportunity Category
A field located on the Grant Opportunity Properties screen within Grants.gov. The Opportunity Category field values include Discretionary, Mandatory, Earmark, and Continuation. The Opportunity Category field was added to the site to assist Grants.gov with aggregating opportunities and application packages for public and private displays on the site. For example, there are links that show grant opportunities and packages recently posted to the site. Those opportunities and packages with a category type of Earmarked or Continuation will not show up on these public listings.
Optional Forms
Optional forms are the forms that can be used to provide additional support for an application, but are not required to complete the application package.
Organization
A grant applicant who is submitting a grant on behalf of a company, state, local or tribal government, academic or research institution, not-for-profit, or any other type of institution.

Outlays or Expenditures
Charges made to project or program, which may be reported on a cash or accrual basis.

Password
A code used to gain access to Grants.gov along with a username. Good passwords contain letters and numbers (e.g.,Virtue7) and must not be found in any dictionary.

Personal Property
Property of any kind except real property. It may be tangible, having physical existence, or intangible, having no physical existence, such as copyrights, patents, or securities.

Point of Contact (POC)
An individual who is designated as the person responsible for authorization and maintenance of information on behalf of a SAM registrant, coordinating communication among organizations.

Prefixed Filename
Attachment filenames may appear verbose because many are prefixed to include the form name, field name, unique number, and attachment name (attachment name that was entered by the applicant) as one entire filename. Not all attachments are prefixed exactly the same, but you will be able to recognize the filename entered by the applicant by reading through the entire line of the filename text.

Prior Approval
Written approval by an authorized awarding agency official evidencing prior consent.

Profile
Applicant information stored in the Grants.gov system for the purpose of identifying a user.

Program Income
Gross income earned by the recipient that is directly generated by a supported activity or earned as a result of the award.

Project Costs
All allowable costs, as set forth in the applicable federal cost principles (see Sec. 74.27), incurred by a recipient and the value of the contributions made by third parties in accomplishing the objectives of the award during the project period.

Project Period
The period established in the award document during which awarding agency sponsorship begins and ends.

Recipient
An organization receiving financial assistance directly from an awarding agency to carry out a project or program.

Recovery.gov
Federal website established in order to accomplish the mission set out in the Recovery Act, and provide information for the public to monitor the progress of the stimulus package.
Recovery Act
See American Recovery and Reinvestment Act (ARRA) of 2009.
Research and Development
All research activities, both basic and applied, and all development activities that are supported at universities, colleges, hospitals, other nonprofit institutions, and commercial organizations. Research is defined as a systematic study directed toward fuller scientific knowledge or understanding of the subject studied. Development is the systematic use of knowledge and understanding gained from research directed toward the production of useful materials, devices, systems, or methods, including design and development of prototypes and processes. The term research also includes activities involving training of individuals in research techniques where such activities utilize the same facilities as other research and development activities and where such activities are not included in the instruction function.
Role Manager
The person listed as the point of contact for a specific grantor agency or subagency. This person will receive any email notifications about application submissions, depending on the option selected in the agency's profile
SIC Code
Being replaced by the NAIC code, a code that was used to classify business establishments.
Stimulus Package
See American Recovery and Reinvestment Act of 2009.
Subaward
An award of financial assistance in the form of money, or property in lieu of money, made under an award by a recipient to an eligible subrecipient or by a subrecipient to a lower-tier subrecipient. The term includes financial assistance when provided by any legal agreement, even if the agreement is called a contract, but does not include procurement of goods and services nor does it include any form of assistance that is excluded from the definition of award.
Subrecipient
The legal entity to which a subaward is made and which is accountable to the recipient for the use of the funds provided.
Supplies
All personal property excluding equipment, intangible property, and debt instruments as defined in this section, and inventions of a contractor

conceived or first actually reduced to practice in the performance of work under a funding agreement.

Suspension

A post-award action by the awarding agency that temporarily withdraws the agency's financial assistance sponsorship under an award, pending corrective action by the recipient or pending a decision to terminate the award.

Synopsis of Funding Opportunity

Summary information extracted from or based on the funding opportunity announcement that is electronically posted at the government-wide website known as Grants.gov/Find. The search tab includes a direct link to the funding opportunity announcement or includes an uploaded copy of the funding opportunity announcement.

System for Award Management (SAM)

SAM validates applicant information and electronically shares the secure and encrypted data with the federal agencies' finance offices to facilitate paperless payments through Electronic Funds Transfer (EFT). The SAM stores your organizational information, allowing Grants.gov to verify your identity and to pre-fill organizational information on your grant applications.

System Requirements

Computer functionality and programming that is required in order for a specific program to operate.

Termination

The cancellation of awarding agency sponsorship, in whole or in part, under an agreement at any time prior to the date of completion.

Third-Party In-Kind Contributions

The value of non-cash contributions provided by non-federal third parties. Third-party in-kind contributions may be in the form of real property, equipment, supplies and other expendable property, and the value of goods and services directly benefiting and specifically identifiable to the project or program.

Trading Partner Identification Number (TPIN)

An identification number. The restricted access number assigned by SAM to the main SAM point of contact who manages information for the SAM registrant.

Unobligated Balance

The portion of the funds authorized by an awarding agency that has not been obligated by the recipient and is determined by deducting the cumulative obligations from the cumulative funds authorized.

Upload

Transferring data (usually a file) from the computer you are using to another computer.

USA.gov
The official web portal of the United States Government, created to improve U.S. Government interactions with the public by offering links to every federal agency to help website visitors quickly find information to the services they seek. USA.gov features links to every federal, state, local, and tribal government agency.
User Guide
A well-indexed, comprehensive guide to reference information about Grants.gov.
Username
The ID (plus password) that allows access into the Grants.gov system and application package submission.

Source: Grants.gov

References

American Grant Writers Association (AGWA).

APA Style: The Publication Manual of the American Psychological Association (2009), 6th Ed.

Blitch, D. W. (2012). "Grant professionals: Profession retention and Length of Service Rates." *Journal of the Grant Professionals Association, 10(1)*: 24-34.

Budget (2015). White House Budget FY2015, Retrieved from: http://www.whitehouse.gov/omb/budget/Overview

Dillehay, J. & Skinner, S. (2012). "Key skills and behaviors of successful grant professionals." *Journal of the Grant Professionals Association, 10(1)*, 72-82.

Donnell, J. and Sheldon, J. (2004). *Writing Style and Standards in Undergraduate Reports.* Glen Allen, VA: College Publishing.

Einhorn, J. (2013). "The power of persuasion: The sustainability of externally funded projects in higher education after funding expires." *Journal of the Grant Professionals Association,* 11(1), 14-26.

Grant, C. and Tomal, D. (2013). *How to Finish and Defend Your Dissertation: Strategies to Complete the Professional Practice Doctorate.* Lanham, MD: The Rowman and Littlefield Education, Inc.

Grant Professionals Association (GPA).

Janssen and Jodi Pearl. (2009). "The compensation differential between female and male members of the American Association of Grant Professionals." *Journal of the American Association of Grant Professionals, 4(1)*, 25-36.

National Endowment for the Humanities (NEH).

O'Neal, V.S. (2008). "The truth about grant writing certification." Retrieved from http://www.families4lifeinc.org

Rajan, R.S. (2014). "Meaningful data for learning in the arts." *Strategy Papers, Grant Professionals Association, 1(3)*, 1-5.

Reynolds, C.F., Martin, C., Brent, D., Ryan, N., Dahl, R.E., Pilkonis, P., Marcus, M.D., and Kupfer, D.J. (1998). "Postdoctoral clinical-research training in psychiatry: A model for teaching grant writing and other research survival skills and for increasing clarity of mentoring expectations." *Academic Psychiatry, 22(3),* 190-196.

Sisk, A. (2011). "How critical is training?: Impact of a semester-long proposal writing course on obtaining grant funding." *Journal of the Grant Professionals Association, 9(1),* 66-77.

Smith, N.B. and Tremore, J. (2008). *The everything grant writing book: Create the perfect proposal to raise the funds you need* (2nd ed.). Avon, MA: Adams Media Corporation.

Sokolow, J. A. (2009). "How to help reviewers evaluate your government grant proposals quickly and effortlessly." *Journal of the American Association of Grant Professionals*

Sridhar, A. (2009). "Grantsmanship and the university: Five strategies for grant professionals working with faculty." *Journal of the American Association of Grant Professionals, 7(1),* 9-15.

Tomal, D. (2010). "Action research for educators." Lanham, MD: Rowman & Littlefield, Inc.

Index

About the Authors

Rekha S. Rajan is associate professor and program leader for the Grant Writing, Management, and Evaluation program in the division of research and doctoral programs at Concordia University Chicago. She is an arts education specialist, and received her doctorate in music education from Teachers College, Columbia University. As a senior research associate with the Center for Arts Education Research at Teachers College, Columbia University, she co-authored over thirty program evaluation reports. She is the author of the books *Integrating the Performing Arts in Grades K–5* (SAGE) and the forthcoming *Children's Experiences in Musical Theater*.

Dr. Rajan has given numerous workshops on the basics of writing and getting grants, including presentations with the Arts and Business Council of Chicago. She is the recipient of multiple regional and national grants, including the National Endowment for the Arts. She is Co-Program Chair for the Teaching of Evaluation Topical Interest Group for the American Evaluation Association is an active member of the Grant Professionals Association.

Daniel Tomal is Distinguished Professor of Leadership at Concordia University Chicago, River Forest, Illinois. He has been a public high school teacher, administrator, corporate vice president, and professor. He received his BS and MAE degrees in education from Ball State University and a PhD in Educational Administration and Supervision from Bowling Green State University. He has consulted for numerous schools, has testified before the U.S. Congress, and was voted outstanding teacher at

Purdue University. Dr. Tomal has authored seventeen books and over 200 articles and research studies.

He has made guest appearances on numerous radio and television shows such as CBS's *This Morning;* NBC's *Cover to Cover, Les Brown, Joan Rivers,* and *Tom Snyder;* CBN's *700 Club; ABC News;* and WYLL's *Chicago Talks.* He is also author of the following books: *Action Research for Educators,* a CHOICE Outstanding Academic Title; *School Resource Management: Optimizing Fiscal, Facilities, and Human Resources* (with Craig Schilling); *Human Resource Management and Collective Bargaining* (with Craig Schilling); and *The Teacher Leader* (with Craig Schilling and Robert Wilhite).